BUYING A USED MOTORHOME

*How to get the most for your
money and not get burned*

By Bill Myers

Table of Contents

Introduction

The call of the open road.

The freedom to travel and not be governed by the restrictions of the airlines, hotels and restaurants.

No standing in line for hours with herds of other people, waiting to be rudely searched for contraband – then forced to sit with your knees in your chest while enduring poor service and long delays.

No hotels charging you a ridiculous hundred dollars a night or more to sleep in their lumpy, bed bug infested beds, while they turn away your pets.

No paying twelve dollars for a small bag of nuts from the mini-bar because the hotel restaurant closed an hour before you got there.

Just Say No!

You can forget about having to deal with these kinds of problems and more like them – if you have a motorhome.

Traveling in your own motorhome means you know who slept in your bed the night before – you.

There's no wondering if the people who slept before you in the motel room you just checked into were contagious or if the sheets were changed when they left.

In your motorhome you're in charge of who sleeps in the beds and you know when the sheets were changed.

And you don't have to worry about running out of food or paying exorbitant prices for stale treats from the mini-bar or waiting for cold food from slow room service. In a motorhome, you've got your own fridge and pantry stocked with the foods you like. And with the full kitchen, you can cook and eat whenever you feel like it.

You can forget about hauling your luggage into hotels every night and worrying about what you may have left behind when you check out in the morning.

With a motorhome, your clothes are in your closet, your bathroom supplies in your bathroom and your favorite pillow is on your bed. No packing and unpacking every time you pull off the road for the evening.

And yes, by all means, with a motorhome, you can bring your pets. They'll enjoy the trip and love being with you on the road.

Your motorhome opens the door travel freedom!

It's true. With a motorhome, you can go where you want, when you want, take what you want with you, eat the foods you like and sleep in your own bed every night.

You'll be able to visit interesting places, meet interesting people and have all the comforts of home with you.

No more wondering about what disgusting horrors lurk in that roadside bathroom when you have to go. With a motorhome, you've got your own bathroom – no lines to wait in, no worries about strangers hiding in the stall next to you, or whether the place has ever been cleaned.

With a motorhome, these worries go away.

But there is a problem with motorhome travel.

It's very addictive!

Once you get used to the worry free lifestyle of having your own food, bed and bathroom traveling with you, it can be difficult to enjoy traveling any other way.

Whether the motorhome you choose is a simple Class B camping van or a Class A outfitted like a rolling palace, the adventures you'll have can become memories you'll cherish for a lifetime.

And contrary to popular belief, you don't have to be wealthy to own a motorhome. In fact, using the information in this book, you should be able to find and purchase a very comfortable and reliable motorhome, often for less than the price of a late model used car.

In this book, you'll learn how to choose the right motorhome one for you, how to avoid overpaying for it, how to laugh at dealer prices and how to avoid the expensive mistakes newbie motorhome buyers often make.

You'll learn how to know when you've found a good deal and when to walk away regardless of the price.

You'll see how to find the best deals on motorhomes, the questions to ask the seller before traveling to view a coach, and the answers that'll tell you to stay away.

You'll also find tips on how to quickly inspect a motorhome, how to research and negotiate the right price, and what to do when you finally find one you want to buy.

This book covers all this and more. Along the way, I share with you some of my experiences, both good and bad, of buying and selling motorhomes.

I hope you'll find this book informative, easy reading and entertaining. After you've read it, you'll be ready to find the motorhome of your dreams, at a price within your budget.

Bill Myers
billmyers@gmail.com

Camping at City of Rocks, New Mexico

Motorhome Classes

As you begin your search for the perfect motorhome, you'll discover that motorhomes are categorized into three distinct classes.

These classes relate to the way motorhomes are constructed, and are used to quickly identify the general size and features you can expect in each motorhome class.

Almost all motorhome sellers and dealers will list their motorhomes by these classes, and it's important for you to know what the different classes are, and what they mean in terms of size, price and driveability.

So let's get started by defining the different motorhome classifications.

Class A – these are the larger bus style motorhomes built on commercial truck chassis.

They are the rolling palaces of motorhomes and usually have the amenities of an upscale condo or apartment. They'll have full size appliances (even a washer and dryer), and often have multiple slide rooms. Some will have two bathrooms, even a fireplace and dishwasher.

Class A Motorhome

Class A motorhomes range in length from 25 to 45 feet. Some are powered by front gas engines, while the larger ones are powered by rear diesels (referred to as diesel pushers).

Even though these motorhomes are quite large, they can be surprisingly easy to drive. Many are built on air-ride chassis and seem to float down the highway.

Prices for used Class A motorhomes start at around $10,000 (for older ones without slides), and starting at around $18,000 and going up you can usually find a relatively late model used one in good condition.

Class C – these are mid sized motorhomes built on a cut-away van or truck chassis, typically the size and shape of rental moving trucks.

A distinguishing feature of the Class C motorhome is the bunk compartment over the drivers cab area.

Four Winds Class C motorhome

Class C motorhomes range in size from 22 feet to over 30 feet, and are typically designed and furnished to meet the needs of the family traveling with small children.

Because they are built on a van chassis, the driver's controls are similar to those found in an SUV or pickup truck, and are not as intimidating as the controls found in a Class A.

Prices for a new Class C start at around $48,000. Used Class C's in good condition can be found starting at $15,000 and going up.

Most Class C motorhomes are gas powered, although some diesel models are available.

Class B – these are smallest motorhomes, built on a standard passenger or work van chassis. Sometimes referred to as a 'camping van', class B's have evolved from simple campers into quite elegant and well appointed units, often costing as much or more than a Class A or Class C.

Class B Motorhome

Even though Class B motorhomes are considerable smaller than motorhomes in other classes, they are fully self contained, and have a kitchen, bathroom and sleeping room for two adults.

Class B motorhomes appeal to those who want something small enough to park anywhere, but have all the amenities of a larger motorhome, including a kitchen, bath and sleeping area.

With all this packed in van sized container, they can be fairly tight inside and are best suited for one person traveling alone or a couple that get along well.

New Class B prices start at around $65,000 and go up quickly. Used Class B's are in high demand and prices reflect the demand. Used Class B's start in the mid teens and go up quickly.

Class B+ – These are similar to Class C motorhomes, but without the bunk area over the cab. This gives the B+ a more aerodynamic shape, a sleeker design, and usually a more upscale interior. They tend to get better fuel mileage than a Class C.

The B+ has the ease-of-driving and parking of the Class B, but offer a lot more room inside. They will be slightly wider, taller and most will have slide rooms.

Class B+ Motorhome – Winnebago View

Class B+ motorhomes are available with either gas or diesel motors, and generally get decent fuel mileage, especially when compared to the fuel mileage of Class A or Class C motorhomes.

The prices for new Class B+ motorhomes start around $70,000 and go up quickly.

Used Class B+ motorhomes retail their value on the used market, and late model, low mileage Class B+ units start in the mid $30,000 range.

These are ideal for couples wanting a low profile motorhome for extended travel, with ease of handling, setup and parking.

Advantages / Disadvantages of each class

Now, that we've covered the basic motorhome classes, let's take a look at the advantages and disadvantages of each class of motorhome.

Advantages of Class A

As mentioned earlier, Class A's are the larger, 'rolling palace' bus style motorhomes.

Being larger, Class A motorhomes typically have:

- More room inside

- Larger kitchens

- Larger bathroom and shower

- More sleeping areas

- Optional bunk beds

- More storage areas

- More towing capacity

- Larger fuel tank

- Larger holding tanks
- Multiple slide rooms
- Larger generator
- Ducted heat and air
- Optional washer and dryer
- Optional dishwasher

If traveling with a number of people, or planning to stay at a single location for a long period of time, a Class A motorhome can be a good choice.

Disadvantages of Class A

There are some disadvantages to owning a large Class A motorhome. These include:

- More challenging to drive on narrow roads, difficult to maneuver in parking lots and crowded city streets
- More difficult to get into gas stations, shopping centers
- Lower fuel mileage (7 to 9 mpg is typical)
- Restrictions in some state and national campgrounds that have motorhome length restrictions
- Due to more systems and features, higher maintenance costs
- More expensive tires (a full set of tires for a Class A can cost several thousand dollars)
- Due to limited parking space or zoning restrictions you may not be able to store at your home.

- You may want a tow vehicle so that when you reach your camp site, you have another vehicle to drive to local attractions

- Rapid depreciation of resale value

With all these disadvantages, you might think I would recommended against buying a Class A motorhome. And in some cases I would.

But if you travel with four or more people and plan to spend a lot of time camping, or will be full timing it, a Class A might be the perfect choice for you.

Because prices of used Class A motorhomes have fallen so dramatically, it is possible to find some amazing deals – as long as you know what to look for (we'll cover that in later chapters).

If you do want one of these rolling palaces, be sure to drive one in traffic and on the highway before you get in too deep. You may discover it's more than you can handle. Or you may find it fits your driving style perfectly.

Advantages of Class B Motorhomes

Class B motorhomes are the small camping van motorhomes that are quite popular these days with baby boomers and empty nesters traveling without children.

Being smaller, Class B motorhome advantages include:

- Easy to park

- Easy to drive

- Easy to maneuver on tight city streets, mall parking lots, sports events

- Better fuel mileage

- Will fit in almost all campgrounds

- Stealth camping a possibility

- Low maintenance costs

- Can be repaired at most auto repair shops

- Can be used as a second car

- High resell value

Roadtrek 190 - Class B motorhome

Disadvantages of Class B Motorhomes

- Limited space inside
- Small bathroom

- Small kitchen

- Limited storage space

- Limited sleeping area, narrow or short beds

- Tight headroom – not for tall people

- Limited access, duck your head to get in

- No slide room (except in newer models)

- No leveling jacks

- High purchase price

Even with all these disadvantages, Class B's are the most popular motorhomes today. Especially those built on the Mercedes Sprinter chassis with the diesel motor – because they get such high fuel mileage.

Because Class B's are so popular and because they can be used as second vehicles, they retain very high resale value. Even units 15 years old can demand higher prices than larger, newer and more luxurious Class A motorhomes.

Still, due to the very limited interior space, Class B motorhomes are not the best choice for all, especially those traveling with more than two people.

But if you have your heart set on a Class B, the good news is you can find older ones in very good condition starting at around $18,000. But due to high demand, these sell quickly.

In a later chapter, I'll show you where to look to find deals on Class B's.

Advantages / Disadvantages – Class C

Class C motorhomes fit half-way between the large size of Class A motorhomes, and the small camping van size of Class B's.

Due to the larger interiors, Class C's are quite popular – especially for families traveling together.

Class C motorhome

Advantages of a Class C

- Much more interior room than a Class B camping van

- Easier to drive, easier to park than Class A

- Larger bathroom than Class B

- Larger kitchen than Class B

- More sleeping areas than Class B

- More storage areas than Class B

- Lower cost of maintenance than Class A

- Slightly better fuel mileage than Class A
- Often have one or more slide rooms
- Engine and transmission can be repaired by most auto shops
- Lower cost to purchase, new or used

Disadvantages of Class C

- Cab overhanging bunk area decreases aerodynamics
- Fuel mileage typically 9 to 11 mpg
- Handles like a large truck, can be stiff riding
- Can be difficult to drive in windy conditions
- Older units are prone to water leaks along overhead cab seams
- Longer units can experience handling problems
- Lower resale value than Class B's

While Class C's don't have the sexy curb appeal of Class A's or Class B's due to their boxy styling, they do have plenty of room inside for a family, and after minor suspension upgrades can handle well on the road.

Because Class C motorhomes have lower resale value and very fast depreciation, there are many opportunities to purchase late model units with low mileage at very attractive prices.

If you're interested in a used Class C, you should be able to find older ones in excellent condition for under $18,000, and brand new ones starting at just under $50,000.

Advantages / Disadvantages – Class B+

Class B+ motorhomes are actually Class C's without the overhanging cab bunk area. Because they are essentially Class C's, they have the same advantages / disadvantages of a Class C, except in one area.

Winnebago View - Class B+ Motorhome

Because Class B+ motorhomes do away with the cab-over bunk area, they are **more aerodynamic**, which results in slightly **better fuel mileage** and much easier handling in winds.

Another advantage of doing away with the overhead bunk is the **elimination of a major source of water leaks** and wind noise found in Class C motorhomes.

But doing away with the overhead bunk area means less storage space and fewer sleeping areas.

Perhaps the biggest disadvantage of Class B+ motorhomes is their price. They are usually priced quite a bit higher than Class Cs, due to better build quality and high consumer demand.

Because they are among the 'most wanted' motorhomes, Class

B+'s tend to hold their resale value longer than Class A's or Class C's.

If you have your heart set on a Class B+, you should be able to find older ones in good condition for prices starting just over $18,000. For really nice newer ones, prices start in the mid $30,000's.

Which motorhome class is best for you?

On paper, when you compare all the advantages / disadvantages of the different classes of motorhomes, it would look like Class C motorhomes would have the most going for them.

They have more room inside than a Class B, are easier to drive than a Class A, and are significantly less expensive to buy than either Class A or Class B motorhomes of similar model years.

Because there are plenty of used Class C's on the market, you can usually find a great deal on one without much trouble. In fact, you can often purchase a brand new or slightly used Class C for half or even a third of the price of a smaller Class B 'camping van' or B+.

But a Class C motorhome may not be the best choice for everyone. They do have their disadvantages, including rapid price depreciation and potential for water leaks around the seams.

How about a Class B?

If you are looking for something easy to drive that can be parked just about anywhere, a Class B might be a good choice. But only if you don't mind having very cramped quarters, a small bathroom and limited storage space.

The Class B vans do look sleek and stylish on the outside, and can attract admiring looks from just about everyone – especially from owners of larger motorhomes.

But in return for the smaller size and sleek looks of the Class B, you give up a lot of space inside.

In a Class B, the bathrooms are very compact, often smaller than even the most cramped airline bathroom. And more often than not, you have to 'assemble' the bathroom to use it. Usually by pulling sections of it away from the wall.

Sleeping areas will be sparse, with narrow or short couches that fold into a bed. And don't expect much room to store your gear or your bedding.

If you're taller than six feet, plus-sized, or travel with a companion, you're definitely going to feel cramped in most Class B's.

Still, for some people, a Class B is the perfect choice.

Maybe a B+?

If you like the smaller size of the Class B, but want more inside room, a real bathroom, more storage space, without the boxy look of a Class C, a Class B+ may be exactly what you need.

In the B+ you get the sleek aerodynamic styling of the Class B in a coach that is slightly wider and a bit longer than a camping van.

Inside, your choices can run from the spartan look of an older Trail-lite or Chinook, to the more luxurious appointments of a Coach House Platinum.

A Class B+ is the perfect choice for those who want more room than a camping van, but don't want to manhandle a boxy truck-like Class C down the highway.

The great combination of small outside size with a surprisingly large interior feel, has resulted in Class B+'s becoming the current second most sought out motorhome style (after B's.)

As a result of this demand, resale values of Class B+'s remain high.

Still, if you know what to look for and where to look, you can find really good condition older model Class B+ units for $16,000 and up.

Maybe a Class A?

If you are looking for a motorhome you can live in for months on end, or even full time, a Class A motorhome might be in your future.

Many Class A motorhomes are built with the full time resident in mind and are designed to have the features of an upscale condo.

You'll find large double-door refrigerators, large kitchens with a pantry, bathrooms with showers – even clothes washer/dryers!

You'll usually sleep more comfortably in a Class A, due to quiet zoned heating and air, and king or queen size beds.

You'll also find cavernous amounts of storage, with cedar lined closets, his and her dressers, overhead cabinets, and huge basement storage in the outside compartments.

Most Class A's have multiple flat screen TVs, elaborate entertainment systems, and are a joy to spend time in.

With all these amenities, you'd expect Class A motorhomes to be expensive. And they are – if you purchase a new one.

But buying used, you can often find top-of-the-line units with low miles for under $25,000. You can find older, less luxurious models with prices starting around $15,000.

In later chapters, I'll show you how to find these great deals on Class A motorhomes.

What to Choose?

When it comes to choosing the right class of motorhome, only you can decide what will be best for your own needs.

But just in case you're wondering, here is my opinion:

- For two adults traveling without children, a Class B+ is a great choice. Easy to drive, easy to park, ideal for day trips and room for two people.

Class B+ Motorhome

- For a family on a budget, a Class C is a good choice. More sleeping areas, more storage room, dedicated dining area, larger kitchen and bath. Easy to drive, relatively easy to maintain, and least expensive to purchase.

Class C Motorhome

- For upscale travel on long trips with extended stays, a Class A can be a good choice. Much more room inside, nicer bathroom(s) and bedrooms, luxury amenities, and basement storage areas. A bit more challenging to drive and park, plus you will need to tow a second vehicle or be prepared to hike, bike or rent cars to get around.

Class A motorhome

- For one person traveling alone, or a couple who don't mind sharing cramped quarters, a Class B might be right. Especially if looking for something to use as a second vehicle. Not recommended for extended camping or for more than two people.

Roadtrek 190 Popular - Class B Motorhome

Should You Buy New or Used?

When it comes to buying a motorhome, one of the biggest questions is whether to buy new or used.

While some people would never consider buying a used motorhome, there are plenty of others who would never buy a new one.

The truth is, there are advantages and disadvantages either way you go.

Advantages of buying new:

- When buying new from a dealer, you aren't buying someone else's problem – except when there are defects or build quality issues from the factory.

- When buying new, you get a limited warranty which should cover most manufacturing problems – but often you'll have to wait weeks or months to get repairs under warranty

- When buying new, you can usually arrange instant financing through the dealer – if you have good credit

- When buying new from a dealer, you usually get a full walk-through of the motorhome showing you how to use all the features

- When buying new from a dealer, you'll often get extras such as free campground memberships and travel vouchers.

Disadvantages of buying new:

- When buying new from a dealer, it's easy to pay way too much. Dealers price their units high and expect you to bargain with them for a much lower price. If you aren't a good negotiator, you can end up paying thousands more than you should.

- When buying new, you'll lose at least 15% of the motorhome sales price in depreciation the moment you drive it off the lot.

- When buying new, you'll pay substantially more – often as much as 70% more – than for a similar make and model motorhome just a three to five years old.

- When buying new, you will be the one who discovers problems with the motorhome and it will be you who has to take it in to get them taken care of. And yes, new motorhomes do have problems.

- When buying new, your choices are often limited to whatever brands the dealer carries and the units he currently has on his lot.

- When buying new, you may have to travel many miles to visit larger motorhome dealers that have wider selections, better prices and better financing terms.

Advantages of buying used:

- When buying used, you can expect to pay a substantially lower price for the same make and model of a new motorhome. Often, you'll find three year old motorhomes will be priced 50% to 70% less than a new one of the same make and model

- When buying used, you have far more choices in make, model, year and price range, especially if you use the internet to search.

- When buying used, you can often find the exact motorhome model with the specific features you want (IE., rear queen size bed, with kitchen slide on Ford E-450 chassis and Ford V10 motor).

- When buying used, you'll often find motorhomes with expensive after-market upgrades you won't have to pay for (like steering stabilizers and suspension upgrades).

Disadvantages of buying used:

- When buying used, there may be expensive hidden problems with the motorhome that won't be covered by any warranty.

- When buying used, you have to rely on the word of the seller about the history and general condition of the motorhome. It is an unfortunate fact that many sellers will be less than truthful about the condition and history of the item they are selling.

- When buying used, you may find motorhomes that have odors from smoking, cooking, pets and general use. These problems usually won't be disclosed in the seller's ads.

- When buying used, the interior and exterior of the coach are likely to show signs of wear and tear.

- When buying used, there may be a need to immediately replace tires and batteries – very common in motorhomes four years old and older.

- When buying used from an individual, there won't be any financing from the seller. If financing is needed, you'll have to arrange that yourself before you buy.

Here's my opinion:

Since getting started with motor-homing twenty five years ago, I've bought two brand new motorhomes, and more than a dozen used ones.

I bought the new ones because at the time, I didn't know any better and thought buying new was the safest way to go.

I was wrong.

I learned that when buying new, you can have just as many problems as when buying used. I also learned that when buying new, if you finance the purchase, you'll likely be 'upside down' on the resale value of the motorhome versus what you owe on it – often for most of the term of the loan. This makes it difficult and expensive if you want to sell or trade it in.

Buying a new motorhome should be a joyous occasion. And sometimes it is. But often, the joy disappears when you discover defects in workmanship, handling issues and costly repairs not covered by warranty.

Even though the new motorhomes I purchased didn't give me the long term joy I'd hoped for, I'm grateful to have gone through the process. Perhaps the most important thing I learned from the experience was how easy dealers make it to buy a new motorhome – as long as you have good credit.

That said, many buyers of new motorhomes are delighted with the experience and are happy with what they paid and the quality of the motorhome they purchased.

Most will have purchased a quality brand of motorhome from a reputable dealer that provides better than average before and the after the sale support.

My advice – **don't rush into the purchase of a new motorhome**. Dealers know you'll be in awe when you first walk into a new motorhome and they also know if they can get you to 'sign on the dotted line', before you have time to go home and think about the purchase, it'll be an easy sale.

Again, **be a reluctant buyer**. Never purchase on the first visit. Do your research and if you do decide to buy, be a tough negotiator.

Buying Used

If you are working with a limited budget and you want to get the absolute best deal on a reliable motorhome, buy a used one from either a dealer or individual.

While new motorhomes are nice, you'll pay a premium price and see immediate depreciation of at least 15% of the selling price the moment you drive the motorhome off the dealer's lot.

If you finance a new motorhome, even if you put 20% down, you'll almost always owe more than the motorhome is worth for the term of the loan.

Here's a typical example:

Regardless of what the sticker price says on the dealer's lot, you can expect to get the motorhome for 15% to 25% off the list price.

On a motorhome with a list price of $100,000 you can expect to bargain the dealer down to around $80,000.

You'll feel good that you got such a great deal – but the reality is all dealers work the same way – 15% to 25% off the list price on most motorhomes on their lot.

If you put 20% down ($15,000) on a $80,000 motorhome, you'll owe $65,000, which can be financed over 15 years.

Your payment will be about $570 a month, and even after five years, you'll still owe about $50,000 on that five-year-old motorhome.

The problem is, that motorhome which you bought new and is now five years old won't be worth anywhere close to the $50,000 you still owe on it.

But if you bought used . . .

If instead of paying $75,000 for a new motorhome, you found a five-year-old used one of the exact same make and model, you likely would be paying around $35,000 for it.

If you put the same $15,000 down, and paid $350 a month, it would be paid for in five years.

Here are the numbers:

If you bought a new motorhome with a sales price of $80,000, at the end of five years you would have:

- Paid $20,000 down

- Made 60 payments, totaling about $33,000 ($21,000 in

interest)

- And still owe close to $50,000 on the loan.

If you bought used, at the end of five years you would have:

- paid $15,000 down
- made 60 payments, totaling $18,248 in payments ($3,000 in interest)
- and owe nothing. You'd own the motorhome outright.

As you can see from the above calculations, buying used can save you a tremendous amount of money.

If you are savvy buyer, you can do even better than our calculations above.

A Safe Buying Strategy

When it comes to searching for and buying a motorhome, whether new or used, abide by these three rules and you'll have a much better chance of ending up with something you can enjoy for years to come.

First rule – Condition

Condition is always more important than price

There is no such thing as a 'bargain' motorhome if it is in poor condition. If advertised as 'needs work', or 'unfinished project', or 'as is' – be very wary.

If a motorhome has not been well maintained, it can easily need $5,000 to $15,000 in repairs and upgrades. Sometimes a lot more.

If the previous owner has left it uncovered and hasn't been checking on it, the motorhome could have developed a water leak in the roof or seams or animals could have gotten in and chewed the wiring or plumbing.

Water intrusion is a motorhome killer. It can cause rotten wood in the ceiling, walls and floors and often is a home for deadly black mold.

A motorhome with soft spots in the roof, delaminated sidewalls, mold or soft spots in the floor won't be a bargain at any price – even if offered for free.

If rats or squirrels have gotten into the wiring or plumbing, it could cost thousands to repair – assuming the damaged wires and pipes can be gotten to without tearing out walls or floors.

If the motorhome wasn't winterized before freezing temps, the plumbing lines could have burst and the water pump frozen, requiring costly repairs.

This is why **condition of the motorhome always trumps price**. If the previous owner didn't care enough to keep the motorhome in good condition, walk away.

You can't afford to fix someone else's problems.

Second Rule – Driveability

Driveability is more important than price or floor plan

Some motorhomes, even some new ones, are very difficult to drive at highway speeds. They'll wander down the road, going from one lane to another with little regard for driver's steering input.

The rear end will feel like it has a mind of its own, not tracking in the same line as the front tires. It'll feel like its moving into another lane. You'll check your side mirrors and it'll look like the rear of your motorhome has pulled out into the adjoining lane with intentions to pass you.

Some motorhomes will porpoise – the front will dive and the

rear end will lift, like a porpoise swimming through the water. It'll do this continually at highway speed, making it difficult to handle while making your passengers sea sick.

Other motorhomes will have four inches of free play in the steering wheel, requiring you to constantly correct the steering to maintain a semblance of going straight.

Others may suddenly dart to the left of right without any input from the driver. While others will have a severe shake in the steering wheel and wobble in the tires at certain speeds.

All of these problems and other like them, do exist in certain models of motorhomes. In fact, if you follow the forums at RV.Net, you'll see one of the most frequently asked question is, 'how can I get my motorhome to handle better?'

Unfortunately, there is no easy answer to solving handling problems.

Sometimes, it can be as simple as adjusting tire pressure and getting a front end alignment. But more often than not, it involves spending thousands upgrading shocks, adding a steering stabilizer, air bags, replacing tie rod ends, adding a stronger sway bar and more.

And even after doing all this, in some cases, the poor handling and driveability issues will still exist.

Most sellers of motorhomes won't tell you about driveability issues. Most will tell you their unit handles just fine. They'll even tell you it drives like an SUV. And sometimes, what they say is right. Their motorhome handles great and does drive like an SUV.

But the reality is, you'll never know until you drive it yourself at highway speeds. That's when you discover the problems.

If, while driving at 60 to 65 mph, you find it difficult to keep the coach in your lane, or find you have to have both hands on the wheel while constantly correcting the steering, this won't be the coach for you.

When it comes to driveability, if you or your spouse is afraid to drive the coach or feel unsafe while driving due to the way it handles or how much effort you have to put in it, you won't drive it much. You'll either keep it parked or you'll want to sell it.

That's one reason you often see motorhomes for sale with unusually low miles. In some cases, the motorhomes have handling issues so severe, the owners were afraid to drive them and kept them parked.

The good news is not all motorhomes have handling issues. Some are easy, even fun, to drive.

That's what you want – an easy-to-drive motorhome. Don't buy anything else. Find out about handling first hand, by taking a test drive, before you make an offer.

If the handling is not to your satisfaction, walk away from the deal.

Third Rule – Floor plan

Floor plan is more important than price

When it comes to enjoying a motorhome, you want one that is easy to spend time in while you are parked, whether at a campground, a roadside park, or a relative's driveway.

This means the motorhome should have room for everyone you plan to travel with, room for all the gear you need on the road, and room for your pets and their gear.

You want the ceiling throughout the coach to be high enough so you don't bump your head. You want the entry doors to be well placed and easy to use.

You want the bathroom to be large enough and easy to get to and use – whether parked or on the road. (Check this when the slides are in.)

You want the beds to be long enough and comfortable to sleep in. You want enough beds for everyone you are traveling with. Maybe you want bunk beds. And room to store bedding materials.

You may want a table to work from, whether for computer work or hobbies. Or just for meals.

All these considerations and more are part of the floor plan of your motorhome and whether they are to your liking or not will make a huge difference in how much you enjoy your motorhome.

For example, I bought a motorhome with a rear door. Not a side door, but an entry door on the back side of the motorhome, above the rear bumper.

At the time, I didn't see anything wrong with it having the coach entry over the rear bumper.

But the first time I camped, I discovered that going in an out the rear door meant I was stepping out into the bushes *behind* the campsite.

The rear door also meant a long hallway was needed through the coach. This required the floor plan designers to reduce the size of the bathroom to less than half the width of the coach, making it smaller than most airplane bathrooms.

The rear door also meant I couldn't put a bicycle rack on the rear trailer hitch. Because if I did, it wouldn't be able to open the rear door. For the same reason, I couldn't tow anything if I wanted to use the rear door.

The rear door presented other problems as well, enough that I soon sold the motorhome and bought a different one – with a side door.

It's for reasons like this that the floor plan is an important consideration when looking for the right motorhome.

To get the right floor plan, make a list of what you want and don't want as far as interior layout, and use the list to eliminate coaches that simply won't work for you.

To summarize

When looking for a motorhome, use this as a quick guide to eliminate coaches from consideration:

❑ **Overall Condition** – search for units that are in fine or excellent condition. Walk away from those that need work, are unfinished projects, have sat unused for years, have been neglected or show any sign of water leaks or just haven't been kept up.

❑ **Driveability** – search for units that are easy-to-drive. Don't take the seller's word. Find out yourself by driving. Keep in mind that some coaches, even new ones, are dangerous to drive, tiresome to handle and can involve spending thousands trying to resolve handling issues.

When you test drive a motorhome, take it out on the highway and get it up to 60mph. If you have to keep a death grip on the wheel to keep from crashing, walk away from the deal, no matter the price.

❑ **Floor plan** – make a list of your floor plan's 'must haves' and 'must avoids'. Use that list to quickly eliminate coaches with floor plans that don't meet your needs.

The Importance of Seat Time

True story – the first time I bought a motorhome I had never actually driven one. I'd visited several motorhome dealers and walked through many Class A motorhomes while imagining how great it would be to take one of these big boys camping.

Without ever having driven one, I had convinced myself that I wanted to buy one. But the high prices on these new units were holding me back.

Then late one Friday afternoon, while looking at a motorhome on dealer lot, a salesman asked me, "what if I could put you in this brand new Class A motorhome for $5,000 down and $400 a month?"

That was far less than I was expecting to pay, so I said, "If you could do that, I'd probably buy."

A few minutes later, we were in the salesman's office, where he wrote up an offer and took it to his boss.

After a short wait, the salesman came back and said, "My boss says we can do this deal if we bump the payment up by $50 a month and if you agree to buy today."

Now mind you, I hadn't driven the motorhome at this point. In fact, I hadn't driven any motorhome ever! But like a lot of first time buyers, I was caught up in the emotional pull of owning a new motorhome.

So I took the deal. We shook hands, and the dealer had my wife and I pose in front of our new motorhome for a photo.

I was pretty proud of my purchase. I had gotten what seemed like a great deal on a brand new motorhome. I didn't even have to wait for the dealer to prep the unit. It was ready for me to drive off the lot.

My wife drove our car back home and I settled into the driver's seat of our new motorhome thinking about how much fun I was going to have with my new purchase.

Getting back home required me to get on Florida's I-75 at rush hour, but I wasn't worried. I figured driving the big motorhome wouldn't be much different than driving a car. Sure, it was wider, longer, and weighed a lot more than a car, but still how hard could it be to drive?

With a high degree of confidence in my driving ability, I guided my motorhome out of the dealers lot, onto city streets, blissfully unaware of what lay ahead.

I took the on-ramp to I-75, got the motorhome up to speed, merged into traffic, and held on tight.

That's when I discovered something I wish I had known before I bought my new motorhome.

Due to a combination of short wheelbase and soft suspension, this particular motorhome was almost impossible to keep in a straight line when going more than fifty miles per hour.

I could line up the front wheels with the white lines of my lane in the highway, but no matter how I steered it, the rear wheels would either be on the shoulder or in another lane of traffic.

When I got the rear wheels going the right way, the front would wander to the left or right – regardless of how I steered. The motorhome wouldn't remain in its lane.

Drivers on both sides of me were signaling their displeasure – either by blowing their horns, or using hand signals.

I could understand their feelings, I would have felt the same way had I been in a car behind or beside the motorhome I was driving.

Eighteen very stressed out miles later, I took the very first off ramp and eased my way back home sticking to less traveled side roads. My confidence in my ability to drive a motorhome on the highway had been blown.

During that short drive, there were several times I was sure I was going to die in violent collision with either concrete road barriers on the right, or high speed 18 wheelers sucking me into their path as they passed on the left.

It was one of the most frightening experiences of my life. Driving a brand new motorhome on the interstate shouldn't have been like that.

I assumed the problem was my driving skill and not the fault of the motorhome. After all, it was brand new. And it drove well in town, at slow speeds.

Not wanting to give up on it, I decided it was important to learn how to drive the motorhome on the highway. It had to be something I was doing wrong.

So a few days later, I took the motorhome out on several short test drives, getting on the interstate, driving to the next exit and getting off.

Each drive produced the same results.

Once the motorhome was going more than fifty miles an hour, it wouldn't track straight. The back-end would either be on the shoulder or a different lane than the front.

I tried everything I knew, but nothing helped. I eventually gave up and took the motorhome to another dealer and traded it in on a different one.

When the dealer noticed I had only clocked three hundred miles since purchasing it, he said, "We see a lot of these. People buy them because they look good and are priced right. But they are really hard to drive unless you spend thousands upgrading the suspension."

On the trade, the dealer paid me wholesale for my almost new motorhome and I paid retail for the one I replaced it with. I lost quite a bit of money on the trade. But I was happy. I may have lost money, but I didn't lose my life in traffic due to an ill handling motorhome!

From that very expensive experience, I learned a very important lesson:

Buying Lesson #1:

NEVER EVER buy a motorhome without first driving it on an interstate highway at cruising speed.

The fact is, not all motorhomes handle well. Some can be quite treacherous – especially on the highway.

So no matter how nice they look on the dealer's lot, no matter how much leather they have in the driver's seat, nor how nice the granite counter tops are, the thing might just be impossible to drive.

And if it's difficult to drive, <u>you</u> don't want to be the one that gets stuck with it.

So always take any motorhome you are considering on a test drive. Not just a short trip around the block. Drive the motorhome on an interstate at highway speeds. And to make it more interesting, do a test drive on a windy day.

Motorhome Test Drive Checklist

When you do your test drive, check these items:

❑ Does the motorhome have plenty of power?

❑ When you turn corners, how far does the back end swing into other lanes?

❑ Does the steering feel firm?

❑ Does the steering require constant correction?

❑ Does the motorhome wander all over the road?

❑ Is there a 'wiggle waggle' when large trucks pass?

❑ Do you feel porpoising when you go over dips and bumps?

❑ Do you have to maintain a 'death grip' on the steering wheel to stay in control?

❑ Do you hear lots of rattles or squeaks?

❑ Is there a lot of wind noise?

❑ Do you have a clear view behind and beside the motorhome as you drive?

If, as a result of your test drive, you fear for your life – don't buy that particular motorhome!

Your goal when test driving a motorhome is to find one you'll feel comfortable with and will be confident driving for many hours on end.

Little things that might not seem important during the test ride can be a major nuisance or safety issue later on when you take long trips.

If you find yourself struggling to retain control of the motorhome during a test drive, pass on that motorhome.

There are plenty of others to choose from. Many will be pleasurable to drive, even on long trips.

The point is – before you fall in love with any particular Class or style of motorhome, get some seat time in several motorhomes.

Doing so will help you decide what kind of motorhome you want, and what kind you want to avoid.

How not to get burned

Over the years, I've owned more motorhomes than I can count. Class A's, B's, B+'s and C's.

I've bought motorhomes new and used, from dealers and individuals. And in most cases, after using and enjoying the motorhome, I've been able to sell them for a nice profit (or at least a minimal loss).

Doing this, I've learned many important lessons. Of these, one of the most important has been . . .

If you don't want to get burned when buying a used motorhome:

☐ **buy the right motorhome**

☐ **from the right person**

☐ **at the right price!**

If you can do that, your motorhome buying experience will be much more enjoyable.

When you buy the right motorhome from the right person at the right price, there's a pretty good chance that when you get ready to sell it, you might get all your money back, even make a small profit.

But if you purchase the wrong motorhome, or pay the wrong price, or buy from the wrong seller, you may end up overpaying for something you won't enjoy owning and will have a difficult time reselling.

For that reason, it's worth looking for the right motorhome, from the right seller at the right price.

In the next chapter, I'll show you how to do that.

Buying the right motorhome

After buying and selling motorhomes for several years, I've learned the right motorhome to buy is the one **people with money will want to buy when you get ready to sell it**.

That kind of thinking drives my wife crazy.

She tells me,"Why worry about who will want to buy it when you get ready to sell it? Get a motorhome you'll enjoy now and don't worry so much about selling it later on."

And she's probably right.

You should get a motorhome you'll enjoy now – unless of course, you don't plan to keep it forever.

But more often than not, people who buy motorhomes don't keep them forever. They trade them for newer ones or ones that have features missing from the one they currently own. Or they downside to a smaller unit. Or an upgrade to a larger one.

And because of that, it does pay to think ahead and consider how easy it'll be to sell when you decide you want a different one.

In my case, I know I'm only going to keep a motorhome for a year or so. Then I'll get the urge to sell it and look for another one. So when I start looking at motorhomes to buy, I look for models that people with money will want to buy when I get ready to sell it.

Checklist for buying the right motorhome:

❏ **Is a 2004 model or newer** – newer motorhomes have newer technology. More reliable and more fuel efficient engines and transmissions. Up-to-date safety features. Modern fixtures and appliances.

And from a psychological point of view, it's a whole lot easier to sell something with a 20 in front of the model year instead of a 19.

❏ **Has less than 45,000 miles** – while most motorhomes can easily do 150,000 miles before major mechanical work is needed, getting one with fewer than 45,000 miles usually means it can go longer before major service is required.

With lower initial miles, you can drive it ten or fifteen thousand miles, and it'll still be a low mileage motorhome when you get ready to sell.

❏ **Has more than 10,000 miles** – motorhomes that have suspiciously low miles often mean the motorhome was so difficult to drive that the owner was afraid to drive it, and just kept it parked.

Motorhomes that have sat unused for a long period of time will almost always require expensive service to get all the parts working again.

This service can include replacing fuel pumps, belts, batteries, tires, brakes, brake lines and a carb rebuild on the house generator.

I've been through this with a motorhome that sat unused for two years. It was inexpensive to buy but cost a lot to make road worthy. Initial purchase price was under $10,000. But I had to spend another $5,000 before it was road worthy.

From that experience, I learned it was better to buy a motorhome the previous owner drove often enough that he found any defects or problems, and fixed them early on.

❑ **Has great curb appeal** – I tend to buy motorhomes that have great curb appeal. Even though they may be ten years old, they often look new, and tend to attract serious interest from people who want to buy a motorhome.

More times than I can count, I've been approached by people in parking lots who ask if I'm interested in selling the motorhome I'm driving. Mainly because they like the way it looks.

That's the kind of motorhome I like owning. The kind that attracts buyers – even when it's not for sale!

❑ **Is from a manufacturer with a good reputation** – Winnebago, Fleetwood, RoadTrek, Pleasureway, Leisure Travel, Coach House, and other motorhomes from well known builders are always easier to sell than those from builders with no name recognition.

Avoid motorhomes from manufacturers you've never heard of, or who have bad reputations (see the chapter in this book about doing research on brands).

❑ **Is extremely clean inside** – the condition of the interior of a motorhome can tell you a lot about how it's been used and taken care of.

If the interior is dirty, smells bad, has spots on the carpets or damage to walls and woodwork, you can be sure the motorhome hasn't been taken care of.

If the inside is clean and looks fresh, it usually means the owner took pride in keeping the motorhome maintained.

❑ **Has no body damage** – the condition of the exterior of the motorhome also tells you a lot.

If there are dents, scratches, missing parts, cracked windows, doors that don't open, panels that don't line up – you can be certain there are problems with the coach.

If the owner hasn't bothered to take care of the outside, he probably hasn't kept up with the required service and maintenance, and that could mean expensive repairs ahead.

❑ **Has no rust** – rust can be a serious problem, especially in Class B camping vans that have mostly metal bodies. If a motorhome has visible rust, it most likely has more rust that you can't see. Just walk away from it.

❑ **Has manufacturer's books and manuals** – having the books and manuals for a motorhome makes it easier to learn how to operate the systems in the motorhome. Having those books and manuals also makes it easier to sell the motorhome later on.

❑ **Is the kind of motorhome people want to buy right now** – the demand for specific types of motorhomes changes over time. For a long time, the larger Class A motorhomes were the most sought after.

These days, Class B's and B+'s are the ones that have the highest demand. People want smaller motorhomes. And because of that, those who own large Class A's are finding their trade in values have gone down quite a bit.

The good news is this means you'll find some great deals in used Class A's, but it also means if you buy one, you can expect the resale value to go down – unless demand for used Class A's goes back up.

Right now, the highest demand is for Class B and Class B+ motorhomes. So much so, that some used ones are selling for more than their original new price.

My opinion on buying the right motorhome

In my opinion, the best motorhome to buy right now if you plan to resell it later, is a ten-year-old or newer Class B or Class B+ with 40,000 or fewer miles on it.

This assumes you and your traveling companions will fit in the small size of most Class B and B+ motorhomes.

If that is the case, then these are the best to buy right now with resell in mind.

But the problem with this strategy is there are so many other people are looking for late model, low mileage, Class B's and B+'s, that finding ones with good prices has become a challenge.

Still, if you know where to look and what to look for, and take your time, you can find good deals on used Class B and B+ motorhomes.

If you are on a tighter budget or need something larger than a Class B or B+, you might want to take a look at Class C's. There are lots of used ones on the market, and many are available at bargain prices.

Same is true with the larger Class A's. The used market is flooded with Class A's, and it definitely is a buyer's market for these. You can often find excellent deals for well under $20,000.

But when it comes time to resell, the Class B's and B+'s will be the ones that sell the quickest and retain their value the longest.

Buying from the right person

Just as important as buying the right motorhome, is buying from the right person.

When it comes to finding the right person to buy from, use the following:

Perfect Seller Checklist

This checklist helps you find the perfect person to buy your motorhome from.

❑ The perfect seller is usually an older person, often retired, who purchased the motorhome new, and who currently owes nothing on it and has clear title.

❑ The perfect seller has taken meticulous care of the motorhome throughout its life, and has kept the service up-to-date.

❑ The perfect seller drives the motorhome at least once every two weeks, keeps the batteries charged, and makes sure all the systems are operating properly.

❏ The perfect seller is usually facing a change in his or her life, and the motorhome no longer fits in.

He's either gotten too old to drive, has no reason to travel, or is moving to a new home where he is not able to store the motorhome and is selling for that reason.

❏ The perfect seller doesn't trust doing business on eBay, and when he took the motorhome to his local dealer to try to sell it, he was offered and embarrassingly low price. Rather than sell to the dealer, he is now advertising his motorhome locally in the newspapers, or on the local Craigslist.

In summary, the **perfect seller** has a great condition motorhome on which nothing is owned, has a clear title, has meticulously maintained the coach and has a good reason for wanting to sell it quickly.

Find someone like that, and you'll be heading in the right direction for a great deal.

So, you're probably thinking the 'perfect seller' is going to be hard to find.

And they can be, unless you live or search in an area where they have lots of perfect sellers.

A good example is the retirement areas of Florida.

Many retirees come to the state, buy a motorhome and use it for several years. Then due to lifestyle changes, often involving health issues or moving to a new home, they put their motorhome for sale.

Perfect sellers like this are not limited to just Florida retirement communities. You can find them in other retirement areas as well, including many southern states, especially Arizona and Texas.

Not only are these southern retirees often perfect sellers, their motorhomes are not being used or stored in the rust belt states – which usually means they are rust free and haven't been exposed to severe winter weather, freezing pipes and salted roads.

Even if you don't live near the retirement areas of Florida, Arizona and Texas, it can be well worth your while to concentrate your searches in those areas (especially the west coast of Florida), to find the best deals on motorhomes from perfect sellers.

Sellers to avoid

Just as there are *perfect* sellers, there are certain kinds of sellers you'll want to avoid.

These include:

❑ **People who owe more on their motorhome than it is worth.** They'll need to sell their motorhome for at least their loan payoff amount, which is often many thousands more than the retail value of their motorhome.

These people are 'upside down' on their motorhome value to loan, and there's not much you can do for them – unless you want to pay more than the motorhome is worth – and I don't recommend doing that!

❑ **People who have lived in their motorhome full time** – especially in disaster situations (after hurricanes, floods, tornadoes, etc).

Living full time in a motorhome can quickly wear out appliances, damage upholstery, leave cooking and other odors and result in moisture problems from condensation (breathing and showers).

No matter how good a deal you're offered, you really don't want a motorhome that has been a full time live-aboard camp for disaster survivors.

❑ **People who sell repo, flood damaged, theft recovery and salvage title** motorhomes.

Never buy a salvage title or flood damaged motorhome – it'll create a lot of trouble and cost your money. With a salvage title, when it comes time to sell, you won't find many buyers. And any that you do find will expect to pay a bargain basement price.

❑ **People who have traveled with lots of unruly children.** While some children are well behaved angels, some are not.

They can flush scissors down the holding tanks (true story), hide gummy bears in the walls, throw up on the furniture – and do things that leave smells, stains and problems you really don't want to deal with.

❑ **People who smoke** – you'll never get the smell of tobacco smoke out of a motorhome. Unless you can find someone who also smokes, you'll have a hard time when you try to resell.

❑ **Dealers who price their used motorhomes far above retail** and won't budge on the price. Most dealers price motorhomes $10,000 above retail, and unless you know how the game works, you'll overpay.

❑ **People who know nothing about the motorhome they are selling**. Often they'll be selling for a relative or a friend and can't tell you anything about the history or problems of the unit they are selling.

In some cases this can work in your favor. But you'll be buying blind – with no service or repair history and other important details from the previous owners.

❑ **Craigslist scammers who list motorhomes they don't own and don't exist**. They'll email you a very convincing story about being in Iraq and the motorhome being stored at a military base.

If you pay their low price, they'll give you directions to the motorhome. But this is always a scam. The motorhome doesn't exist, and the seller will cheat you out of your money.

As a general rule, if a Craigslist motorhome ad doesn't include a phone number, it is a scam.

There are a lot of people you probably don't want to buy motorhomes from. That's why taking the time to find the perfect seller can be worth the trouble.

Even it if means you have to travel to Florida, finding the perfect seller with the right motorhome is usually worth it.

Related to this, I have a friend who lives in Oregon who travels to Florida to buy motorhomes he takes back to the west coast to sell for a substantial profit.

He's able to do this because in Florida retirement areas where there are a lot of motorhomes for sale, asking prices tend to be substantially lower than in other parts of the country.

Even factoring his cost of travel, he can typically make a $10,000 profit on motorhomes he brings back to the west coast.

If you live in an area with a limited supply of quality used motorhomes for sale, you'll almost always see higher asking prices. That's why if you want to find the best deals, you'll want to look in areas where there are lots of used motorhomes for sale.

In those areas, you'll find more to choose from and generally at lower prices.

Buying at the right price

Now that you've learned about buying the right kind of motorhome from the right kind of seller, you'll want to know about buying at the right price.

So how do you come up with the right price for any particular model motorhome? You start by . . . .

Knowing the market

Knowing the motorhome market means you do a bit of research so you can learn what different makes and models of motorhomes have recently sold for.

For example, if you are interested in a buying a 2006 Winnebago View Class B+, you'd want to start by seeing what these have recently sold for on eBay.

You're interested in the <u>actual selling price</u> on eBay, not the asking price of units that didn't sell or didn't get any bids.

To do this, visit eBay, log into your account, and search for 'Winnebago View' in eBay motors.

When the results show up, look in the left hand column, find the 'search options' category, and click the 'completed listings' link.

This will show recent completed auctions for the item you searched for.

Look for auctions that actually ended with a sale, and you'll get a good idea of the real world value of that particular model of motorhome.

But that's not necessarily the price you would want to pay. You'll want to pay *less* than what similar units are actually selling for on eBay.

Paying less than what a unit would sell for on eBay gives you the confidence that if for some reason you don't like the coach and decide to resell it quickly, you can get all or most of your money back by listing it on eBay.

But the only way to know what a specific model of coach would sell for on eBay, is to search eBay before you make an offer.

Doing that kind of search before you call a seller about a particular motorhome is part of the process of getting a good price.

In addition to finding out what similar models are selling for on eBay, I always search to see if there are lower priced units available on Craigslist.

To do this, I do a nationwide search on Craigslist using http://www.searchtempest.com/ . I choose the 'recreational vehicles' category at SearchTempest and enter the motorhome model I want to search for.

The search results will show all the matching units for sale throughout the country, and you can see the price variations state by state.

You'll likely discover that asking prices are quite a bit lower in places like Florida than the Pacific Coast (California, Oregon & Washington).

Sort through the listings that interest you, and you'll start seeing a pattern of price trends.

Knowing these trends will help you come up with what you consider to be a good price for the coach you want.

When I find well priced models, I generally print out the page and take it with me to use as a negotiation tool when I visit a seller who has the same make and model motorhome.

Getting more out of Craigslist

Because I use Craigslist to do a lot of research, I've found ways to help me use it better.

First, I search my local Craigslist, for the makes and models of motorhomes I'm interested in buying.

When the results page comes up, I put a check in 'include nearby areas', and then click 'update search'.

Then I choose 'save search'.

When you do this, you'll be asked to log into your free Craigslist account and confirm that you want to be notified by email when matches to your search criteria are found.

I typically have twenty searches going on at a time, using different keywords and spellings of the items I'm looking for.

For example, when looking for Class B motorhomes, I set Craigslist searches in the RV+camp category for these keywords:

• Roadtrek

- Class B
- Van
- Pleasureway
- Leisure Travel
- Coach House
- Cruiser
- Airstream
- Ford
- Camper

When listings are posted including any of the above words, Craigslist notifies me by email about the listing.

And because of this, I'll usually find out about the listing before others see it, and that gives me an advantage when looking for items that are hard to find or are in limited supply.

It also gives me an easy way to follow asking prices of the units I'm tracking.

If you are tracking a specific make, model or type of motorhome, you may want to try setting up email notifications at Craigslist for the keywords that best describe what you are looking for.

Staying within your budget

Most motorhome buyers will want to set a maximum amount to spend before they begin their search.

The good news is no matter how low your maximum amount is, you should be able to find a decent motorhome to fit your budget.

For example, I recently purchased a nice Class B+ motorhome

from a retired 'perfect seller' who had grown too old to drive.

He told me I was the only one who had responded to his local newspaper ad, and even though his asking price was $13,500 – he agreed to sell to me for $7,500 (see photo below).

I paid just $7,500 for this motorhome!

We were both happy with the deal, and he even called me the next day to tell me he had extra cables and a table that belonged with the motorhome that I could have if I would just come by and pick them up.

The point is, there are always decent motorhomes in your price range if you're willing take the time and use the tools to look for perfect sellers.

Another thing to remember is that many sellers will advertise a price way above what they'd really take for the unit from a cash buyer.

That means even if the price shown is twice what you'd pay, it never hurts to make a lower offer – but only after viewing the coach and making sure it is the one you want.

Example: I saw a really nice American Cruiser Class B camping van listed on a consignment lot for $19,500.

From my research, I knew that price was at least $6,000 too high.

The owner who had consigned it wanted much less, but the consignment lot manager wanted to hold out for an unrealistically high price.

After several months of no offers, the unit finally sold – for $10,500 – almost 50% less than the original asking price!

This is not unusual. Sellers often set a 'pie in the sky' price, hoping someone not knowing any better will pay it.

But this can backfire on the seller. When they set a crazy high price, many potential buyers are scared off and won't even bother to call.

The seller gets no calls, no offers and eventually realizes the price is way out of line and is willing to come down quite a bit. But by then, many potential buyers have moved on to other units and are no longer interested. That makes it a good time for you to go in an offer a realistic price – if the unit meets your requirements.

Avoiding the wrong price

As you begin your search for a motorhome, you'll likely visit many motorhome dealers lots. That's a good thing.

By visiting dealer lots, you'll be able to walk though different models, see the different floor plans and features and get an idea of how dealers price used motorhomes.

But you've got to be careful. Being surrounded by great looking motorhomes on a dealer lot, you risk being seduced by the 'dream of owning' and before you know it, you'll find yourself in a salesman's office writing up a contract and paying too much.

Before that happens, know this.

- Motorhome sales people are there to sell you a motorhome at a nice profit for the dealer.

- They work for a commission and it is in their best interest to get you to pay the highest price for the unit that they can.

- No matter how much a salesperson tries to make you think he's your friend, he is not. He is just doing his job, trying to sell you a motorhome.

Don't get me wrong. There is absolutely nothing wrong with a salesperson trying to do his job. He is paid when he makes sales. So he's going to try to convince you to buy. That's the way the commission sales business works.

As long as you understand this, and know that the salesperson works for the dealer and not for you, you'll be okay. In fact, you may find this relationship can work to your advantage.

See, motorhome sales people are paid to bring offers to their boss, the sales manager. And just because a motorhome has a price sticker on it, it doesn't mean you have to offer anything close to the asking price.

Dealers expect you to negotiate the price downward. Because of that, they generally set their asking or sticker price at least 15% higher than they expect to sell it for. Some set it for 25% higher, or even more.

That way, they can let the customer negotiate a big discount off the asking price, and the dealer still makes the profit they wanted.

So if you want a great deal, ignore their asking price and know beforehand what the motorhome is really worth based on the research you've done on eBay and Craigslist.

If you decide you want the motorhome, you'll know what to offer the seller – a price below what the coach would sell for on eBay.

If the salesman tells you he'd be embarrassed to give your low offer to the boss, tell him to do it anyway. That's his job.

If the dealer needs to move inventory, it might be your lucky day. They might accept your offer just to meet a sales quota.

I've actually had this happen to me.

Here's how it went down.

There's a large and very well known RV dealer in my area, and twice a month I visit to check out their used inventory. During one visit, I found a used Class B Mercedes motorhome I was interested in.

I knew these were in high demand, and sell quickly on eBay, so I asked the salesman who was following me around the lot about it, and he said it was sold.

In fact, he said, "It sold within an hour of being on the lot. First person who saw it bought it."

According to the salesman, even before they cleaned it up, a customer had fallen in love with it, and offered the full asking price of $49,000.

When I visited the same RV lot two weeks later, the motorhome was still there. I asked the salesman about it and he said, "Yes, it's sold, but the deal hadn't closed yet."

I told him it was the kind of motorhome I was looking for, but I wouldn't offer anything close to the asking price.

When he asked how much I'd offer, I told him $30,000, and he laughed.

"No way my boss would accept that. That's $19,000 below what he's already accepted."

I said, "No problem. Just thought I'd make an offer." Then I started to walk away.

Then the salesman said, "Wait. Let's write it up and see what the boss says."

We wrote up an offer, contingent on my driving the motorhome and it passing my inspection. And then the salesman took the offer to his boss.

About ten minutes later, he came back with a smile on his face. He said the boss called the person who said they would purchase it and discovered the buyer had changed their mind – without informing the dealer.

So it really wasn't sold.

The dealer had seen several other deals fall through that week, and decided he wasn't going to lose another one. He agreed to take my low ball cash offer, but only if I would do the deal before the day ended.

I agreed and was happy to buy at my price – $15,000 less than the exact same make and model motorhome had sold on eBay two days earlier!

Yes, you can find great deals – even at dealer lots!

The point of this is . . . if you have a budget and have done the research and know what specific models of motorhomes are selling for in the real world, you'll know the right price to pay.

You won't be bullied by a dealer or a seller into paying too much, and you won't be afraid to start by negotiating from your price, instead of negotiating down from theirs.

Narrowing down your choices

One of the problems when it comes to finding and buying the right motorhome is there are just so many makes, models and floor plans to choose from.

For example, on eBay, you'll typically find over a thousand motorhomes up for auction, with prices starting at under a thousand dollars.

On Craigslist, you'll find more than five thousand motorhomes for sale nationwide. And if you check the other resources I mention later on in this book, you'll find another ten thousand used motorhomes for sale.

So with this many choices, what's a person to do?

Here's my advice – build up **walk through time** in as many motorhomes as you can.

By that I mean go out and **walk through** as many motorhomes on dealer lots as you can.

And when you do this, take time to check out the different features in each motorhome.

Create a checklist of the things that are most important to you in a motorhome, and use that checklist to help you eliminate the models that won't work for you.

Here's the checklist I use:

Motorhome features checklist

- **Location of bathroom** – Do you want a rear bath (more room), an aisle bath (usually smaller), split bath, or more than one bath?

- **Size of bathroom** – Is there room to stand up? Is there a bathroom sink? A mirror? A medicine cabinet? Can you sit on the toilet with bumping your knees?

- **Size of shower** – Can you stand up and move your arms around in the shower? Can you easily open and close the shower door?

- **Size of bed(s)** – Is there a bed, or do you have to fold out the sofa. If you have to sleep on the sofa, is it comfortable (most aren't). If there is a bed, is it long enough for you? Can you get up and walk around the bed at night without stubbing your toe or bonking your head on something?

- **Number of beds** – are there enough places to sleep for the people you will be traveling with?

- **Size of kitchen** – Is there enough counter space? Easy to reach microwave? Large enough refrigerator? Enough storage for food and utensils?

- **Refrigerator** – Is it big enough? Enough freezer space?

Does it run on shore power and propane? Is it easy to turn on?

❑ **Amount of closet space** – Is there any hanging closet space? Any place to pack your clothes? Are there enough places to store cameras, computers and other gear?

❑ **Dinette table** – Is there a dinette table? Does it have enough room for everyone to sit? Is there a place to use your computer?

❑ **Couches** – Is there a couch? Does it convert into a bed easily? Does the couch block the walkway when converted to bed? Is the couch comfortable?

❑ **Head room** – Can you walk around without stooping over or bumping your head on the ceiling?

❑ **Walkways** – Can you walk front to back with the slide rooms in? Can your co-pilot leave the passenger seat and get to the back while you drive?

❑ **Entry door head banger** – Do you bang your head when getting into the coach? *(A real problem with many Class B coaches.)* Can you stand up from couches and tables without banging your head on lights or the TV?

❑ **Slides** – Does the coach have a slide? More than one? Can you walk through the coach when the slides are not extended?

❑ **Interior colors** – is dark inside or too bright? Will the colors be popular in years to come?

- **Driving position** – While in the driver's seat can you reach all the controls? Can you see the rear view mirrors? Is there a back up camera? Does the driver's seat feel comfortable?

- **Control panel** – Is there a master control panel? Is it easy to find and use?

- **Entryway** – Is the entry to the coach on the side or in the rear? If rear entry, does this mean when you haul bikes or tow something you can't get out the back door?

- **Outside storage** – Is there room to pack extras you'll be taking with you? Tools, sporting gear, lawn chairs, bikes?

- **Special Feature** – is there a special feature you must have? If so, put it on your list and make sure you don't forget about it when narrowing down your choices.

Learning to look for answers to the above questions as you walk through motorhomes can help you decide which models suit your needs and which don't make the cut.

The only problem when walking through a lot of motorhomes is it is easy to forget which ones you like. For that reason, I suggest taking a camera with you and shooting photos of features you like so you can recall them later on.

While at RV lots, don't limit yourself to walking through just a particular class of motorhome. Doing so can be a mistake.

For example, when I started looking for my first motorhome, I was dead set on a Class A. I wouldn't even consider anything else so I didn't bother walking through Class C's.

Had I started looking at Class C's, I probably would have purchased one instead of a Class A – because at the time, many

Class Cs had all the features I wanted and the prices were much better.

So do yourself a favor. Walk through a lot of motorhomes. Keep mental and even written notes as well as photos of what you like and don't like.

If you find something you really like, ask the sales person to write the make, model and price on the back of his card.

Keep the card for reference and use it to check prices online to see what the unit should sell for.

Do this enough, and you'll narrow your search down to just the right coach for you.

What I look for in a motorhome:

As I've mentioned before, I've bought and sold a lot of motorhomes.

I buy these for personal use and then sell when I want something different or better. Over time, I've discovered that what I (and most other people) want is a motorhome that matches the items on the following checklist:

Motor-home most wanted checklist

☐ **Has great curb appeal**. Looks good and is something you can be proud to own and drive.

☐ **Feels modern** when you step into it. No purple velour on the walls or seats. No puke green shag carpet, no burnt orange refrigerator.

☐ **Has no unusual odors** – no tobacco smells, no food smells, no pets odors, and absolutely no wet, mildewy smell.

❑ **Has a real bathroom**, one that you can stand up in without bumping your head. And a real sink with a vanity.

❑ **Has a real shower** – large enough to stand up and move around in.

❑ **Has a full size refrigerator** that runs on electric and propane. With enough room in the freezer to hold at least six microwave dinners.

❑ **Has a large kitchen area** with enough counter space to prepare food.

❑ **Has a dinette** where you can sit and eat meals or use a computer.

❑ **Has a comfortable couch** with reading lights above and long enough to stretch out on.

❑ **Has a side entry door** – No rear door entry for me.

❑ **Has enough room inside for me and my traveling companion**, with sufficient storage space for all that we carry.

❑ **Is new enough that it has modern safety features** like driver and passenger air bags.

❑ Has **less than 40,000 miles**.

❑ **Is easy to drive**, easy to park, has no squeaks or strange noises, handles well on the highway, in the wind and when big trucks pass by.

❑ **Is not so long or wide** that it is difficult to drive and restricted from some national parks

❑ **Is mechanically reliable** – with wide availability of parts and can be worked on just about anywhere in the country.

When I find a motorhome that satisfies all the above, I can be pretty sure it will be one I'll enjoy. And when I get ready to sell it, it'll likely appeal to a lot of potential buyers, and will sell quickly.

Searching for motorhomes online

For the most part, I search for motorhomes using the internet. This allows me to search throughout the country for specific makes and models that meet my search criteria.

Using just a few saved internet searches, I can quickly find the deals I'm interested in and avoid the tens of thousands of ones that don't meet my criteria.

Here's how I go about it.

After walking through motorhomes on dealer lots, I make a list of the makes and models that interest me.

As I narrow down my selection list, I visit the discussion forums at http://www.rv.net/forum/ and do a search on the models I'm interested in.

From that search, I can see what current and previous owners of those motorhomes have to say about them.

Often the owners will report a recurring problem, lack of manufacturer support, or issues that would rule out the motorhome as one to buy.

When I find one that most current owners warn others away from, I mark that model off my list.

If I find one that all owners seem to love, I'll move it up nearer the top of my 'wanted' list.

By doing this kind of research, I learn which makes and models to avoid, as well as any problems and issues to watch out for when I go see a specific model of motorhome.

After doing my research, I'll end up with a short list of models I'm interested in, and I'll start searching for those.

I start with these sites:

Online Motorhome Listing Sites

- **www.eBay.com** – I check the 'motorhomes for sale' section of eBay almost every day to see what people are bidding on different motor homes – especially the models I'm interested in.

  I usually don't buy motorhomes on eBay, as the auction bidding process can drive prices higher than I want to pay.

  For me, eBay is a good place to see what people are paying for motorhomes and a good place to sell motorhomes. But not always the place to get the best deal when buying.

- **www.craigslist.com** – I've found a number of good deals using Craigslist. But I also find lots of fraudulent offers for non-existent motorhomes from scammers.

  My experience has been if a Craigslist list ad for a motorhome doesn't include a phone number, it very likely is a scam.

If the seller isn't willing to talk to you on the phone, or won't tell you where you can see the motorhome, or tells you he is deployed over seas, or needs to sell the motorhome to raise money for a wedding, it's probably a scam.

If you learn to recognize and avoid the scam listings, you can sometimes find a great deal on a motorhome being offered by a perfect seller on Craigslist.

- **http://www.searchtempest.com/** – As mentioned earlier, I use this free website to search all Craigslist locations nationwide or by region or state for specific keywords.

- **http://rvs.oodle.com/** – A site that compiles motorhome for sale listings from a large number of classified ad and dealer web sites. You can search by model as well as by distance from your home and you can set it to notify you when a new ad is posted matching your search criteria.

  Often, Oodle will have motorhomes that don't show up on eBay or Craigslist.

- **http://www.rvtrader.com/** – Filled with mostly dealer listings, but does includes listings by individuals. Asking prices are typically higher here, usually full retail and more, but deals can be found.

- **http://www.campingworld.com/rvsales/** – Lists new and used motorhomes found at Camping World locations throughout the US. Full retail prices, but you may be able to negotiate a better deal.

- **http://www.roadtrekchapter.org/roadtreks-for-sale** – site where you can find Roadtreks for sale by owner

- **Motorhome for sale groups on Facebook** – over a billion people use Facebook and some of them list their motorhomes there in Facebook for sale groups. If you search Facebook groups for 'RVs for sale', you'll find several groups filled with RV listings from individuals. For example, there's one for Florida RVs at
  https://www.facebook.com/groups/FloridaRVsFSBO/

  Others include:
  https://www.facebook.com/groups/248682128841742
  https://www.facebook.com/groups/606451142707399/

In addition to the above sites, I often search the web sites of large motorhome dealers located within 100 miles of my home. I've found they'll often have motorhomes listed on their sites that aren't listed anywhere else.

As I do my searches, I take note of motorhomes located closest to my home – because it is always a lot easier to visit and do a walk through if the motorhome is near by.

That said, I've driven as far as a thousand miles to check out a promising motorhome and would do it again if I found the right one at the right price from a perfect seller.

Responding to motorhome ads

As soon as you start looking for motorhomes, you'll discover thousands of them being advertised on the web, in your local newspapers, and in motorhome magazines.

Learning how to sort through these ads is important if you want to find the right deal for you.

The first step is learning how to quickly weed out the deals to avoid. Doing this will make it easier to recognize the potentially good deals.

To do this, I use this checklist:

Weeding out bad deals and fraudulent ads

❑ First, I **check to see where the seller is located**. If it is in a rust-belt state, I cross off the ad. Motor-homes that have lived in freezing temps and salted roads usually have too much rust or other weather related issues for me to consider.

❑ Then I **check to see if the seller is an individual or a**

dealer.

❑ **If the seller is a dealer**, I'll go to the dealer's web site to see what other motorhomes they have for sale. While there I'll check out photos of their facilities. Then I'll use Google Maps to get a street view of their location.

With Google maps street view, I can see if the seller is actually a motorhome dealer or someone posing as one. I've found a number of so called 'dealers' are really body shops that rebuild wrecked or salvage motorhomes. Or the seller's listed address is a storage building or mail drop box. If they say they are a dealer but don't have a real dealership, I delete them from my list.

❑ **If the seller is an individual** and the ad doesn't include a phone number, chances are the ad was placed by a scammer trying to get money for a non-existent motorhome.

I usually mark these off my list, unless I'm curious as to what kind of scam is being run.

Usually it's either the 'wedding' or 'military' scam. In both cases the seller tells you he is out of town or overseas, needs money and is selling the motorhome at a very low price.

If you pay him, he'll tell you where the motorhome is so you can pick it up. These are always scams.

Never pay a penny until you've actually seen the motorhome in person, inspected it, taken it for a test drive, checked the title and have negotiated a fair price.

❑ **If the ad looks legit**, I'll get a sheet of paper with my prepared questions on it, and give the seller a call.

❑ When I reach the seller, I follow the outline conversation shown below:

What to ask when calling the seller

====================================

Hi, I saw your ad for the 2006 Coach House motorhome, and I might be interested in it.

Is it still for sale?

If it is, could you tell me . . .

❑ **Where is the motorhome?**

If the seller can't or won't give a street address where the coach can be seen, it is probably a scam. End the call. That said, some sellers are reluctant to give their home address for privacy reasons. If they agree to meet you to show you the coach in a shopping center parking lot or safe space, it probably is legitimate. In those cases, continue with these questions.

❑ **Do you have clear title?**

❑ **Is the title in your name and in your possession?**

If the seller answers 'no' to either title questions, you'll probably want to end the call. If the seller doesn't have a clear title, he can't sell the coach to you without getting others involved.

But if the answer is 'yes' to both, continue with these questions.

❑ Are there any problems with the coach?

❑ Any leaks or water damage?

❑ Is there any rust?

❑ Has it ever been in an accident?

❑ Any broken or cracked windows?

If the seller answers 'yes' to any of the condition questions, it might be time to end the call. If the motorhome has been in an accident, has rust, leaks or water damage, you don't want it.

❑ Has the coach been smoked in?

If you are allergic to or can't abide with carpets and upholstery that smell like cigarette smoke, you may want to end the call now.

❑ When was the last time it was driven?

If it hasn't been driven within the last thirty days, it may mean it has serious unnoticed or undisclosed problems. A motorhome needs to be driven regularly to keep the systems in tip top shape.

❑ Does the generator start and run?

A generator that doesn't start will usually need at least $500 or more in repairs.

❑ How many hours on the generator?

If the generator has <u>extremely low hours (less than 20 per year)</u>, <u>it may not have been exercised properly</u>. Coach generators should be <u>run at least twenty minutes each month</u>. If the generator has <u>high hours (200+)</u>, it could mean the coach was <u>lived in full time and could have significant wear</u> and tear <u>on appliances and furnishings</u>.

❑ **Does the refrigerator and freezer cool down properly?**

A fridge that doesn't cool is usually a costly repair – figure at least $1,000.

❑ **How old are the tires?**

RV tires should be replaced every five years. A set of six RV tires will cost over $1,000. <u>For Class A's, a set of tires will cost over $2,000</u>.

❑ **How old are the batteries and will they hold a charge?**

Most RVs have at least two deep cycle coach batteries. If they are old or won't hold a charge, they'll need to be replaced. Figure at least $125 per battery.

❑ **When was the last time you took the coach out on a trip?**

<u>A motorhome needs to be driven regularly so that all systems stay lubricated and flat spots don't develop on tires and electrical motors, carbon doesn't build up on pistons, sludge doesn't accumulate in oil and transmission fluids, and rust doesn't grow in the radiator</u>. <u>Ideally, a motorhome should be taken on three or four five hundred mile trips each year</u>.

$$\overline{X} \quad 3,000/yr$$
$$\times 6 \ (2014\text{-}2020)$$
$$18,000$$

$$1,500 \ yr$$
$$\times 6 \ (2014)$$
$$9,000$$

$$\begin{array}{r} 2 \\ 18,000\overline{)38,000} \\ \underline{36} \\ 2000 \end{array}$$

Twice the average

❏ **What kind of fuel mileage do you get?**

Whatever answer you get, expect it to be inflated by 2-4 mpg. Actual mpg will be less.

❏ **When was the last time the oil was changed?**

A seller who has maintained his coach properly will have a pretty good idea when the oil was last changed. If they don't know, it can mean importance maintenance has been neglected.

❏ **Are you negotiable on the price?**

Most sellers will be negotiable. If they are not, it might mean they owe money on it and can't sell it for less. This will make it difficult to buy.

======================================

During the call, I'll write down the seller's answers and if there are no red flags and if the coach is local, I'll arrange a time to inspect and take it for a test drive.

If the coach is not local and if I'm still interested, I'll ask the seller if he can provide more photos, the VIN number, and if possible, a video walk through of the coach.

If he is hesitant to provide more photos, I'll usually pass on the deal.

But if more photos are provided and if they look good, and if the price is within reason, I'll check the VIN using Carfax.com, and if it matches the description of the coach, I'll make arrangements to travel to see it.

But before I do, I do a Google Street view of the seller's location to see if it looks legitimate. Doing so might even show the coach in his driveway.

While it might seem crazy to travel five hundred miles or more to view a motorhome, it can make sense if the motorhome is the exact model you want, in the condition you want, at the price you are willing to pay and from a 'perfect seller'.

For motorhomes far away from my home, I'll usually rent a car from Enterprise (unlimited mileage) and drive to the seller's location. That way, if we are able to make a deal, I can return the rental car locally, and drive the motorhome back home.

If the coach deal doesn't work out, I can drive the rental car back home and turn it in. My only expenses will be my time, the cost of the rental car, and a motel room for the night. This is far less expensive than buying the wrong coach or missing out on a good deal.

If I agree to buy

When it comes to payment, I never travel with cash, as doing so is very dangerous. Instead, I'll make arrangements with my bank before I start my motorhome search to make sure I have funds in my checking account to cover my expected purchase price.

 Then at the seller's location, we'll take the title and go to his bank where I'll pay with a check.

When the bank verifies to the seller that my check will clear, I'll get him to sign the title over to me and I'll drive the motorhome back home – after dropping off the rental car and making sure the motorhome is road worthy.

When it comes to working with banks, you can speak the account manager at your bank and let them you want to purchase a motorhome and ask for help to work out the payment details.

Even if you are getting a bank loan, your bank can often work with the seller's bank to transfer the funds the day of purchase and escrow the title.

Motorhome deal killers

When inquiring about a motorhome for potential purchase, there are a few things that absolutely must be right or you should pass on the deal.

These things are 'deal killers', and you'll want to know about them before you travel to view a motorhome, and definitely before you make a purchase.

Deal Killer Checklist

❑ Seller owes more than the motorhome is worth

❑ Seller doesn't have clear title

❑ Seller needs permission from others to accept price or to sell (IE – MH in a family trust)

❑ Seller says the motorhome has a salvage title

❑ Seller doesn't have possession of motorhome

❑ Seller won't disclose location of motorhome

❑ Seller won't provide VIN – vehicle identification number (useful for pulling a CarFax)

❑ Seller wants payment before you can test drive motorhome

❑ Seller advises motorhome hasn't been started in years

❑ Seller advises electrical components or furniture have been removed (common on theft recoveries and repos)

❑ Seller says motorhome has rust

❑ Seller says there are signs of water leaks in ceiling

❑ Seller says windows are broken missing

❑ Seller says there are soft spots in floor

❑ Seller hasn't owned the motorhome for long, doesn't know its history or anything about previous owners

❑ Seller makes claims that can't be verified or are clearly false

❑ Seller's location is in a suspicious area

❑ Seller claims to be a dealer, but Google maps street view shows otherwise

❑ Seller changes his answers when you ask questions

❑ Seller says to bring cash to an unsafe, unknown location

Any of the above are deal killers. No matter how low the price may be or how good the deal seems, if you hear any of the above, run away from the deal!

Inspection and Test Drive

After you've called the motorhome seller and determined there are no deal killers, you'll want to arrange a time to view the motorhome, inspect it, and if it looks good, take it for a test drive.

I usually try to schedule a viewing earlier in the day, so I have time to do a thorough inspection and take the coach for a test drive. By going in early, I have time to negotiate and complete the sale before the end of the day if I decide to buy.

When scheduling a viewing, I'll ask the seller to plug the coach into shore power and turn on the refrigerator so it can cool down before I arrive.

Then before visiting the seller, I'll search the internet to find similar coaches for sale at lower asking prices, and print the listings to take with me.

Having these comps on hand can help when it comes to negotiating a better price with the seller.

As a general rule, you never want to inspect a motorhome while it is raining. A wet exterior can make even faded paint look good and can hide blemishes or problems you'll want to know about.

The day after a heavy rain is a good time to view – as it will be easier to discover any interior water leaks if they exist.

Of course, the best time to visit a motorhome is when the seller is the most motivated to sell – and that's usually after his ad has been running for weeks with no sale. It could be he has overpriced the unit, and has finally realized his mistake and is willing to deal.

Or it could be the motorhome has problems that no one wants to take on. If this is the case, walk away from the deal.

Or it could be the motorhome is listed for sale in the wrong place, or the ad is poorly worded or the photos don't do it justice.

Whatever the reason, if the motorhome sounds good and you get the right answers to the questions you ask during your call, you'll probably want to go check it out.

Pre-Purchase checklist

After you've contacted the seller and arranged to view the motorhome, you'll want prepare yourself to do a proper inspection and test drive.

To keep from making an expensive mistake, you need to be able to view the motorhome without being so in love with the idea of owning a motorhome that you overlook serious problems with the one you are considering.

This is a common occurrence with people looking for their first motorhome and is the reason dealers often find customers willing to overpay or overlook problems.

The customer falls in love with the idea of owning a motorhome and the dream of traveling the country, and in their rush to become an owner, they become emotionally married to the idea and fail to do a proper inspection.

You'll want to avoid this infatuation, and one of the best ways is to use a pre-purchase check list to help you more clearly understand the pros and cons of the motorhome you are looking at. To make this easier, I've created a simple pre-inspection list you can use.

You'll want to take it, along with these other items, with you when you go to inspect a motorhome:

☐ Ladder

☐ Notebook and pen Take notes on history

☐ Reading glasses

☐ Flashlight with fresh batteries

☐ Small digital camera

☐ Tire pressure gauge with 120 psi range

☐ Small mirror – for looking into hard to see places

☐ Cotton gloves – to protect your hands

☐ Calculator – to add up costs when computing offer

☐ Small tool kit, with screwdriver and pliers

☐ Rug or blanket – to put on the ground when you climb under the motorhome

☐ Walkie Talkie

☐ Refrigerator thermometer

☐ Multimeter

After you arrive on location to view the motorhome, speak with owner to find out about the history of the coach. Let him (or her) tell you all they know. The more they talk, the more information you'll be getting. Every bit of it might be important in learning about the motorhome and the seller's demeanor.

If there are no red flags with what the seller tells you, ask him or her to give you a quick walk-through.

Let the seller tell you about the motorhome as he shows you the features. Point out any potential problems and ask questions about them. Again, let the seller talk.

If after the seller's walk-through, you're still interested in the coach, tell the seller you might be a buyer, and ask if it would be okay for you to go through your check list.

If the seller says 'no' to your inspection request, thank him for his time, walk to your car and leave.

But if the seller agrees, start with an exterior walk-around, checking the following:

Exterior Checklist   ☐ *Mirror Adjustment*

☐ General condition and curb appeal

☐ Accident damage, especially around the rear corners

☐ Cracked or broken windows glass

☐ Signs of fluid leaks anywhere underneath motorhome

☐ Missing or broken mirrors

☐ Low, flat, bald or irregular wear patterns on tires

☐ Flaking or cracked paint

☐ Cracks in fiberglass cladding

❑ Cracked or missing caulk around seams

❑ Seals needing repairing (around cab, roof, corners)

❑ Signs of rust (check generator bottom pan and propane tank as these usually are the first to rust)

If you find problems with any of the above areas, it may not be worth your time to continue. But if the exterior looks good, it's time to check the inside.

As you open the coach door, check to make sure the coach steps (if they exist) extend as they should and work properly. The steps should feel firm when you step on them.

On the inside, check the following:

Interior Checklist

❑ Mirror replaced tile - why?

❑ Floor plan – does it meet your needs?

❑ General condition of furniture and carpet – look for signs of abnormal wear, pet and water damage

❑ General condition of interior ceiling covering – look for discoloration and water spots

❑ Any unusual odors (pet, food, smoke, mildew)

❑ Signs of water intrusion – look for water spots under windows, walls and under seat cushions

❑ Soft spots in the floor

❑ Problems with windows, curtains, missing screens

- Any unusual wear or spotting on couch fabric, or firmness of cushions

- Condition of dinette (if applicable)

 Mirrors by Stove
- Wear and tear of counter, sink, faucets

- Overhead cabinets – open each to check if hinges work properly and to see condition of side walls within cabinets, including signs of water leaks

- Location and size of bathroom – can it be easily accessed when slides are in?

- Condition of toilet – it should be securely mounted in floor, no soft spots around it

- Condition and size of shower – check shower pan for soft spots (indication of rotten floor)

- Location of sleeping areas – check to make sure bed is wide and long enough for your needs

If all the above meet with your approval, continue your inspection by testing the mechanicals of the coach.

To check mechanicals:

Mechanicals Checklist

- Test the generator – it should start easily and run without stumbling. Run it with the coach air conditioner set to high so you can see how it handles a load.

 How many hours   93

❑ Test the refrigerator – place a thermometer in the fridge and leave it there for a few minutes. When you check it, the fridge should be 38 degrees Fahrenheit or lower. The Freezer should be 10 degrees Fahrenheit or lower.

❑ Test the plumbing system – turn the water pump on and flush the toilet. Run both hot and cold water in sinks. Look around toilet and under sinks for signs of leaks. Water pump should turn off a few seconds after you turn off faucets.

❑ Test the electrical system – try all light switches, exhaust fans, air conditioning, microwave, TV, and stereo system.

❑ Test the control panel – check to see that it shows all system and tank levels. Check that each panel switch operates properly.

❑ Test the propane stove – look for signs of rust under stove grates, then light each burner to make sure they all work.

❑ Test the refrigerator in propane mode – it should light easily and stay lit.

❑ Test the couch – see if it folds into a bed. It should open and close easily and have no broken springs.

❑ Check interior windows – they should open easily. The screens should be in good condition.

❑ If there is a slide room, run the slide out to make sure it moves without problems.

If all the above checks out okay, it's time to **check the motorhome running gear**.

❑ Awning

❑ Power Step

❑ Leveling Jacks

❑ VIN #

Running Gear Checklist

❑ Sit in the driver's seat and adjust as needed.

❑ If the seat has power adjustments, test that they work.

❑ If steering wheel is adjustable, test that it works.

❑ Start the motor. It should start easily. Check side mirror to see if signs of smoke from exhaust. There shouldn't be any.

❑ Check that all the dash gauges are operational.

❑ Check that power windows roll up and down without problems.

❑ Check that power door locks work.

❑ Check that dash air conditioning cools down quickly.

❑ Check that remote mirrors operate properly.

❑ If equipped with backup monitor, check to see that it operates properly.

❑ Check the horn.

❑ Operate left and right turn signals. (It helps to have an assistant outside to confirm the lights are working in tandem with the dashboard.)

❑ Check headlights and running lights.

❑ With foot on brake, put motorhome in gear. Listen for unusual noises. Put back in park. Make sure parking brake is set.

❑ Step outside and listen to motor. There should be no unusual noises.

❑ If there are no problems, it is time to check fluid levels and condition of the tires.

❑ Turn the motor off.

❑ Use the hood release to open the hood. Look for smoke or oil on engine or signs of improper repairs.

❑ Pull oil dip stick and check condition and color of oil, using a paper towel.

❑ Check brake fluid level.

❑ Check general condition of belts.

❑ Check under coach for fluids (air conditioner water drip is to be expected).

Since it is unlikely you'll have the expertise to do a full mechanical check of the motor and transmission, if you have concerns or if the coach has high mileage, you may want to get it checked out by a local mechanic.

❑ Visit Service Dept.

Checking tires

Check the general condition of the tires. There should be plenty of tread left, and no cracking along the sidewalls.

To check the build date of the tire, look for a 4 digit number on the tire sidewall. The first two digits indicate the week the tires were manufactured, and the next two digits will be the year.

If you find a code that looks like:

LMLR 5109

It means the tire was built in the 51st week of 2009.

If the date code shows the tire is more than five years old, it is time to replace the tires, no matter how much tread is showing.

If tires need to be replaced, make a note and be sure to factor this in while negotiating a sales price.

Road testing

If you're satisfied with the general condition of a coach and have found no deal killers or mechanical problems, it's time for a road test – but only if you are still interested in the coach.

If you aren't interested, don't waste the seller's time and fuel by taking a test drive. Just thank the seller for his time and leave.

But if you are seriously interested, take a test drive.

Test Drive Strategy

When I do a road test, I usually ask the seller to drive for the first few miles while I sit in the passenger seat. This gives me a chance to see how the coach rides without being distracted by the challenges of driving an unfamiliar vehicle.

It also gives me a chance to see how the current owner treats the vehicle as he drives, and to see if he has problems starting and driving the coach.

True story – I was interested in a Chinook motorhome I found in a RV dealer's lot. After inspecting it and seeing that it was in pretty good condition for its age, I decided to take it for a test drive.

I asked the salesman to drive it the first few miles and we took it out on the highway. As soon as we got up above forty, I watched as the salesman desperately worked the steering wheel side to side trying to keep the motorhome going straight down the road.

After a few miles, he pulled over to the side of the road and asked if I wanted to drive. I didn't. I'd seen enough.

If the salesperson was having a hard time keeping it on the road, it wasn't going to be something for me.

We talked about the handling problems on the way back to the dealer lot and the salesperson admitted it was scary to drive. He said because of that, they were willing to cut the price by several thousand dollars.

But I knew better. If the dealer, with their big repair shop and alignment rack, couldn't fix the handling problems, it sure wasn't something I wanted to tackle on my own. I passed on the deal.

I was happy I had the salesman drive first. It let me see first hand the struggles any driver of that coach would have keeping it on the road.

That's why you want the seller to drive first. To see and hear problems before you take the wheel.

One other thing – some sellers will turn the radio on for the test drive. Don't let them do this. You don't want to hear the radio.

You want to listen for mechanical noises, knocks, bangs, transmission whine, cabinet creaks and cracks and other sounds the motorhome makes. Some of these might indicate problems that need to be investigated.

You might not be able to hear them over the radio – and that's why some sellers will crank up the audio when you go for a test drive. When they do, politely ask them to turn it off.

Then start the test drive.

After the seller has driven a few miles, if there are no major issues, ask for a chance to drive.

When I drive a motorhome for the first time, I'll start on back streets so I can familiarize myself with the handling and braking characteristics of the coach. If this part of the drive goes well, and I'm still interested in the coach, I'll ask the owner if we can take it out on the highway.

If he doesn't agree, I'll pass on the deal right then.

But if he does agree, we'll go out onto the highway and see how well the coach handles at 60 mph.

Ideally, it should handle well, not wander around the road and not be easily disturbed by passing trucks.

While on the highway, test the cruise control. It should be easy to set and should hold the set speed without problems.

Drive on the highway for at least five minutes so you can see if driving the coach requires the two-handed 'death grip' on the wheel, or if the coach can easily be driven one handed. If it takes two hands or continual steering correction, it can mean serious handling problems that can be expensive to repair.

After leaving the highway, check behind for traffic, then test the brakes. Then head back to the seller's location.

If at this point all has gone well, and if you're still interested in buying the coach, it's time to start negotiating the price.

Negotiating the price

If after doing the inspection and the test drive, I'm still interested in the coach, I'll begin by negotiating the price.

Before I start, I'll know from my online research what similar make and model coaches sell for on eBay, and will have printouts of ads for similar units at lower prices than the seller is asking.

Here's how my negotiation typically goes:

Price Negotiation Conversation

Me: I like your motorhome and am interested in it. If we can settle on a price, I'll buy it from you today.

Seller: Sounds good. What price were you thinking?

Me: You've got a nice motorhome here, and it really shows you've taken care of it. But as you probably know, prices on motorhomes have fallen quite a bit lately.

Still, yours is in such good condition, I'm willing to offer you

$XXXX, cash today.

Seller: No way I can go that low. I've got to have at least $XXXXX for it.

Me: A few years back it would definitely be worth that. And you've really taken good care of it. But these days, they just don't sell for that.

I've found others like yours for less than I'm offering you today. (I show the seller some of the printouts I've brought with me.)

I'd rather buy yours than one of the others, but I just can't pay your price.

So what's the best you can do today? For cash?

Seller: The best I can do is $XX,XXX. *(A bit lower than before.)*

Me: Well, that's getting closer. Still a bit above what I can pay.

Me: How about this. I'll meet you half way. We can do the deal right now and you won't have to waste your time with tire kickers and joy riders who don't have the money to buy.

Seller: I really wanted a bit more. I'm sorry, I can't sell at that price.

Me: Well, if you change your mind, let me know. *(I start to walk away.)*

Seller: Wait. If you can do a cash deal today, I'll sell for $XXXX.

Me: That's getting closer, but the best I can do is $XXXX. If you agree, we can do the deal right now.

Seller: I really wanted more. But if you've got cash, I'll do it.

Or

Seller: I can't sell it for that. Sorry.

At that point, we've either made a deal or we haven't.

If we haven't made a deal, I'll thank the seller for his time, give him my phone number in case he changes his mind, and then get in my car and drive away.

I'm never afraid to walk away from a deal. Especially if during any point of the inspection, test drive or negotiation, I start to feel uncomfortable about the seller, the location or the coach. When that happens, I've learned to say, "Sorry, this isn't the right one for me."

When you check out used motorhomes, you'll learn that most won't pass your inspection or won't have the features you want, or won't be realistically priced.

When this happens, just walk away.

Doing so gives you time to do more research and find a better motorhome and to negotiate a better deal.

But when you do find a motorhome that is exactly what you want, at the right price, and from the right seller, be careful about walking away too soon.

These perfect deals usually don't last long.

Example: I recently saw an ad for a late model PleasureWay Class B camping van on my local Craigslist. It was listed for $10,000 below what they sell for on eBay.

Rather than call about it right away, I waited about four hours. Then I called the seller.

He turned out to be one of those 'perfect sellers' I mentioned earlier. Older, retired, bought the motorhome new, and owed no money on it.

He was getting too old to drive, so he priced it for a quick sell. The first person who looked at it, bought it on the spot.

A few days later, I saw the same motorhome on eBay – offered for $12,000 more than it had just sold for locally.

In this case, the early bird definitely got the worm.

That's the way it works sometimes – especially with highly sought after Class B and B+ coaches that are priced right.

The right ones at the right prices, usually sell quickly. If you find one, you may not want to let it get away.

Completing the deal

After you negotiate and agree to a price, there are a few steps you have to take to complete the deal.

I generally follow the items on my:

Completing the Deal Checklist

❑ First, I ask to **visually inspect the title**. I make sure there are no liens on it and the VIN number matches the VIN on the motorhome.

This is when you might discover the year model on the title is one year older than the advertised year model of the coach. This is common and quite legit.

Motorhome builders often buy the chassis they build on directly from the manufacturers (Ford, GM, Chevy, Mercedes, etc), well in advance of building the motorhomes. They'll often be building this year's motorhome on a chassis with last year's date.

The title VIN is for the chassis and it might be a year older than the motorhome itself. This is not a problem. As long as the year on the title isn't more than a year older than that stated by the seller, it usually is okay.

❑ After inspecting the title, I'll **ask the seller to prepare a bill-of-sale**. Since most sellers won't have a bill-of-sale form handy, I'll usually have one with me. I find these on my states DMV web site, and print out copies to carry with me.

❑ On the bill of sale, we'll **enter the required fields** – make, model, VIN, mileage, price, seller's name and address.

❑ I'll get the **seller to sign the bill-of-sale**, and if he has a copier, I'll ask him to make a copy for his records.

❑ Then **for payment**, I'll ask the seller to drive me to his local bank, where I'll write a check to cover the motorhome price. In most cases, the bank can verify the check and give the seller his proceeds.

❑ In cases where the bank can't clear the check immediately, I either **arrange a wire transfer** from my bank, or agree to wait a day until the check clears before I pick up the motorhome.

I always prefer taking possession of the motorhome immediately after I pay – that way I know nothing will change between the time I pay and the time I pick it up.

❑ **Financing** – if you plan to finance a motorhome purchase from an individual seller, you'll want to get pre-approval from your bank or credit union for a specific loan amount before you begin negotiating with the seller. You'll also want to make arrangements with the loan officer so you can pay with a check upon finding the motorhome you want to buy.

❑ **Insurance** – Most states, including the state I live in, require you to have insurance on any vehicle you drive on the road.

I've learned that the quickest and most affordable way to get motorhome insurance is to go online and get a motorhome policy from http://www.progressive.com/rv/

Progressive's motorhome rates are usually significantly lower than other RV insurance providers, and when you sign up online you can print out your required proof of insurance cards immediately.

❑ **Road Breakdown Assistance** – I never drive a motorhome without a Roadside Assistance plan. These will cover you if you have a flat tire, are locked out, or break down on the road and need towing service. There are several plans available from difference services including AAA, but for motorhomes, I prefer the Roadside Assistance plan from Good Sams. You can read about it at https://www.goodsamroadside.com/

❑ **Safety** – For personal safety reasons, never exchange cash or funds except in a safe and secure location. I prefer to make the payment and do the title transfer at either a branch office of my or the seller's bank.

I never give the seller a reason to think I'll be carrying actual cash to his home and if I'm unsure about the seller or his location, I'll ask to meet him with the motorhome in his bank's parking lot.

These days, you can never be too careful when dealing with sellers you find on Craigslist or eBay. For that reason, it is always better to be safe than sorry. If possible, take someone along with you when you go see the motorhome, as there is usually safety in numbers.

Before you drive any distance

After you've purchased your motorhome and taken possession of it, you'll be tempted to take it on the road. But before you do, there are a few things you must do first.

Before you drive away checklist

❑ Before leaving the seller's location **disconnect any shore power cables and water hoses** and securely store them in the coach.

❑ **Ask the seller if he has any other gear that should go with the motorhome**.

Every time I've asked this question, the seller has come up with items they bought for the motorhome and no longer need. Once a seller remembered he had a brand new Tyvek cover (worth $800) for the coach, and he gave it to me.

❑ **Check to make sure all outside compartment doors are**

securely locked. Don't just assume they are locked. Always check.

❑ **Check the air pressure in all the tires**. If the motorhome has sat unused for more than a month, chances are good the tire air pressure is incorrect.

Running on under-inflated or over-inflated tires can be extremely dangerous as well as hazardous to your health.

True Story: My brother was the high bidder on a motorhome auction on eBay and invited me to go with him to pick it up.

At the seller's home, we did a quick inspection of the coach, did a test drive, and agreed to the sale.

After doing the paperwork, my brother asked the seller, "Have you checked the air pressure in the tires recently?"

The seller, who was holding what appeared to be his 3rd or 4th beer of the day, said, "Just this morning, I filled all the tires up with air."

Taking his word on this, we headed back home.

It was a hot August day and our route took us through Tampa, Florida, over the long Sunshine Skyway suspension bridge – which sits several hundred feet above the water.

Just after passing over the bridge, we heard a loud bang as the right rear tire on the motorhome exploded, taking with it the fender flare and some of the motorhome's plumbing lines.

My brother safely pulled to the side of the road, and we got out and surveyed the damage.

The rear quarter panel of the motorhome had been ripped away, the tire shredded, and the bathroom plumbing lines dangled on the ground.

It took us quite a while to find the jack and spare and replace the tire and get the plumbing lines secured. But we got it done.

Before hitting the road again, we decided to check the air pressure in all the tires – and found that the seller had indeed '*filled them up*'.

Even though the tires were rated for a maximum of 70psi, the seller had put more than 120 pounds of pressure in each of them!!!

He'd apparently connected an air compressor and filled the tires until they wouldn't take any more air.

In doing so, he had over inflated the old tires to almost twice their rated capacity.

It was no wonder the tire exploded! It's more of a wonder they all didn't explode.

Had it happened as we were crossing the Sunshine Skyway bridge, it could have killed us both.

From that scary experience I've learned to always carry a tire pressure gauge and always check the air pressure on all tires conform to the coach manufacturer recommendations.

You can usually find these recommendations printed on a sticker inside one of the overhead cabinets inside the coach or on the driver's side door.

❑ After checking the tires, head to the nearest service station and **fill up with fresh fuel.**

On motorhomes that have been sitting for a while, there's no telling how old the fuel in the tank is. By adding fresh fuel, you increase the odds you can make the trip back home without problems.

❑ While at the service station, it's a good idea to **check the oil level, brake fluid level**, and everything else under the hood (if you haven't already done so during your inspection).

❑ At the first chance you get, stop at a legal dump station and **drain the black and gray sewage holding tanks**. Then fill each tank with about a gallon of water.

❑ When you get home, **drain the fresh water holding tank, and sanitize** by refilling with fresh water and adding a cup of bleach for every ten gallons of water.

Then turn on all the faucets and let them run until you smell bleach. Leave the bleach in the lines for a day. Then run the water to drain the tanks and lines, and refill the tanks with fresh water.

❑ With the newly bought coach at home, **spend time cleaning it up**, vacuuming it out, washing and waxing, and repairing any minor problems.

True story – After buying and paying for a used motorhome, I drove it ninety miles home. About half way there, I started smelling a strong odor coming from the back. It wasn't your typical car smell. It didn't smell like engine exhaust, burning oil or hot electronics. It was more of a heavy chemical smell infused with perfume.

The more I drove, the stronger the odor got. My eyes were soon watering from the smell and I had to lower the windows to get some fresh air.

Once home, I spent hours cleaning the coach and looking for the source of the odor. But I couldn't find it. For the next few days, each time I drove the coach, the smell would return. Stronger than before.

Eventually, while chasing down the source of a thumping rattle, I found an open bottle of holding tank fluid wrapped in a plastic bag that had fallen behind the back of a kitchen cabinet drawer.

The bottle would roll around on the floor, thumping on the sides of the cabinet as I drove. With each thump, holding tank fluid would leak from its loosely tightened top, releasing the strong chemical odor I had been smelling.

The coach had been professionally cleaned by the dealer before I purchased it and the bottle hadn't been found (or had been inadvertently left behind by the cleaning crew). No matter how the bottle got there, it presented a major problem that would only get worse over time. Fortunately, I discovered it before too much fluid had been spilled and was able to 'clear the air'.

On another coach purchase, it took me several days to chase down a particularly loud and annoying rattle, only to discover the previous owner's silverware drawer had spilled three forks and a large metal spatula out the back of the drawer and onto the floor below the cabinet.

Each time the coach hit a bump, there would be a cascade of metal against metal noises that sounded like pieces were falling off the coach.

Finding the hidden silverware trove and removing the spatula and forks solved the problem.

These two incidents are good examples of why thoroughly cleaning your new-to-you motorhome is important. You'll often find hidden areas filled with noise makers and other things that when removed or cleaned up, will make the coach much more enjoyable.

Best buys in used motorhomes

With more than 10,000 used motorhomes on the market at any time, it can be difficult to sort out the good from the bad (or not so good).

With that in mind, here's my list of best used motorhome buys:

Used Class A

When it comes to Class A's, stick with the major well know brands. Winnebago, Fleetwood, Coachmen, Forest River, Itasca, Tiffin and others.

While there is no guarantee that these will be problem free, it will be easier to get service and parts for them if needed.

Here are some of my favorite picks:

- **Fleetwood Southwind** (gas) – 1999 and newer with Ford Triton V10. A Consumer Report's best buy, and with good reason. Well made, and built on the very reliable Ford Chassis with the Ford V10 motor. Usually available with one or more slides.

I've traveled thousands of miles in one of these and was very impressed with how well it handled – whether in town or on the highway. Fuel mileage was surprisingly good for the 36 foot model, we averaged 10-11 mpg.

You can find these in good condition with prices starting at just over $14,000. Newer models will cost more, but they do hold up over the long run.

- **Fleetwood Bounder** (gas) – Another solid unit from Fleetwood. Available in both Chevy and Ford powered units. Plenty of room, easy to drive, low maintenance. Usually available with one or more slides.

I've seen an older Chevy powered version of these sell for under $12,000 with less than 35,000 miles and in good condition.

I personally prefer the Ford V10, as it has proven to be a very reliable motor over many years.

- **Winnebago Adventurer** – One of Winnebago's best selling units, the Adventurer is a well built, well outfitted, reliable motorhome. Low mileage, like-new units six to eight years young can be found starting at under $20,000.

Other Winnebago models to consider, include:

Winnebago Journey
Winnebago SightSeer
Winnebago Voyage

Almost all Winnebagos and Itasca (Winnebago's upscale

brand), are decent motorhomes. Well built with good a reputation.

- **Fleetwood Discovery Diesel Pusher** – If you are looking for a high end diesel pusher at a great price, look for a six to eight year old Fleetwood Discovery with low miles, and expect to find one for under $40,000.

  The Fleetwood Discovery is a top-of-the-line luxury diesel pusher, perfect for a family traveling long distance or full timers.

Diesel or Gas?

When looking at Class A motorhomes, one of the big questions is "Should I get a gas or diesel powered unit?"

If considering a thirty-six foot or longer coach, diesel is the way to go. It'll cost you more in maintenance, but the diesel will have the power you'll need to maintain speed and climb hills in larger heavier coaches.

For thirty four foot and shorter coaches, a Ford V10 gas engine will give you plenty of power, with reasonable fuel mileage, and almost no significant maintenance expense.

Smaller Class A's

Most of the major Class A builders have entry level units designed for casual living. These are usually built on the same reliable chassis as their larger units, but with less frills inside. If you don't need granite counter tops and deep pile carpeting, one of these might be right for you.

- **Winnebago Brave / Winnebago Vista / Fleetwood Flair,**

Fleetwood Storm, Forest River FR3 25DS – These are shorter Class As, with more spartan (less luxurious) interiors. Ideal for weekend warriors, tailgating, or small families.

Note: If you want a shorty, be sure to drive it on the highway to make sure it handles well, as handling can be an issue with some shorter Class A's.

Used Class C's

There are a lot of manufacturer's that have jumped into the business of making Class C motorhomes. A few do it well, while some turn out shoddy products that seem to fall apart quickly.

For that reason, I recommend sticking with well known manufacturers that are still in business.

Regardless of manufacturer, you'll want to inspect any used Class C carefully, particularly looking for water leaks near the overhead bunk and around the corner seams.

Be aware that quite a few used Class C's were formally rental units, and I wouldn't recommend buying one of those.

Here are the ones I would look at:

• **Winnebago Minnie Winnie** – Another best seller from Winnebago, well built, well appointed, and reliable. Avoid the extra long ones, as they have substantial rear overhang which affects driveability.

• **Winnebago Access** – Good floor-plan in a shorter Class C. Winnebago built quality and reliability, with decent resell value. I've seen three-year-old, low mileage units sell for less than $25,000.

- **Fleetwood Tioga/Jamboree** – Fleetwood makes decent Class C motorhomes and they sell a lot of them. This means many used ones for sale, with some bargains to be found. Inspect closely and do a real test drive before negotiating price.

- **Coachmen Concord / Freelander / Leprechaun** – Later model Coachmen Class Cs have better quality than the earlier Coachmens, and if you find a good deal on one with low mileage, it might be worth taking a look at.

- **Phoenix Cruiser** – Phoenix makes mainly Class B+ motorhomes, but they are often found in the Class C listings. They have good build quality, nice floor-plans, and when priced right are worth taking a look at, too.

- **Born Free** – Another builder of mainly Class B+ motorhomes, frequently found in the Class C listings. Well built, good reputation for safety and reliability. High resale value.

Used Class B+

As mentioned earlier, Class B+ are essentially Class C's without the overhead bunk. By eliminating the overhead bunk they not only eliminate the major cause of problems in a Class C, you get a more aerodynamic coach which equals better fuel mileage.

Many Class B+'s have all fiberglass, seamless bodies. This reduces chances of leaks, reduces wind noise, and means very little caulking problems to worry about.

When searching for a B+, you'll often find them listed with Class Cs' so be sure to search that classification as well.

My choices with it comes to Class B+:

- **Coach House Platinum** – These are by far the best built Class

B+'s on the market, and as such they have a high purchase price and retain their resale value.

It won't be often that you'll find a great deal on a Coach House Platinum, but sometimes you'll be at the right place at the right time.

I've seen a few seven-year-old models sell in the $45,000 price range, which is a bargain for a Coach House Platinum. (I currently own a Coach House Platinum 232 XL and it is one of the best built and best handling motorhomes I've ever check out.)

- **Winnebago Aspect / Itasca Cambria** – These feel more Class C's like inside, but have the streamlined looks of a Class B+ on the outside. Typical Winnebago build quality and reliability. Prices for used ones in good condition start in the mid twenties and go up quickly. They are ideal for families.

- **Phoenix Cruiser** – Another quality Class B+ builder, Phoenix offers several floor plans from a shorty to a full rear walk around bed. They don't sell huge volumes of them, so used ones are rare, but worth looking into if the price is right.

- **Born Free** – Extremely well built Class B+, designed for two people on the go. The rear door design is not for everyone, but they have all the advantages of a smaller Class B, but offer a larger, more spacious interior. Born Free's generally hold their resale values for a long time. Difficult to find a good deal on a used one.

- **Trail-Lite by R-vision** – This discontinued line of coaches was among the first Class B+ coaches offered. Available on both the Ford and Chevy chassis, with and without slides. Known for their spartan interiors, easy driveability, and low purchase price. When you find one with low mileage for under $18k, you'll want to take a closer look.

- **BT Cruiser** – An affordable entry level B+ with better than average build quality. Well thought out floor plan with full rear bath, full size fridge and decent kitchen area. Find a 2004 or newer in decent condition for under $20,000 and you'll be on the right track.

- **Winnebago View / Itasca Navion** – Built on the Mercedes Sprinter chassis, these hybrids are part B+, part C. Their big claim to fame is the great fuel mileage given by the 5 or 6 cylinder (depending on year), diesel motor.

  These units are equipped with slide, nice floor plan, and generally handle quite well. Strong demand for the better fuel mileage these unit achieve means higher resale value. You'll typically pay an added premium of $10,000 to $15,000 for any motorhome on the Mercedes Sprinter diesel platform.

  Be aware that with any Mercedes chassis motorhome, maintenance costs are higher, parts are quite a bit more expensive, and finding places to service the Mercedes motor can be a problem, especially in remote areas.

- **Chinook** – A true cult classic, Chinook Class B+'s were at one time the most highly desired B+ on the market. Chinook went out of business in 2005, meaning most of the Chinooks on the market are older, and often have higher mileage.

  Chinooks are well built, but the rear door entry does mean a smaller bathroom – which may not suit all. These usually have a premium price, and it can be hard to find a good deal on a low mileage unit.

Class B – Camping Vans

When it comes to Class B camping vans, there are a number of different manufacturers, but all build on the same basic platforms and have similar floor plans.

So when you see any Class B advertised, it is usually a good idea to take a closer look, since these are in high demand.

The most well known Class B manufacturer is RoadTrek. Their 190 Popular on the Chevy chassis is very desirable, as well as the newer models on the Sprinter chassis.

When it comes to prices, anything newer than 2002 will bring the best price and have higher resale value.

Those units based on the Mercedes Sprinter chassis with the fuel sipping diesel motor will have the highest prices and highest demand.

While the gas powered Class B's can expect 13 to 17mpg, the Mercedes Sprinter based B's can get 16 to 20mpg – which many buyers find very appealing with today's unpredictable gas prices.

When it comes to Class B's, here's what you'll find:

- **RoadTrek** – As mentioned above, they are the most well known Class B builder. Their most popular model is the 190 Popular built on the Chevy van chassis. Due to the popularity of this and other Roadtrek models, they retain high resale value – even 15 year old models command high prices.

  Other RoadTrek models include the 170 Popular and Versatile and the 200 & 210s. The 210 is the largest in Roadtrek's Class B lineup and they offer more space inside than the typical camping van conversion.

Roadtrek offers Class B's built on the Mercedes Sprinter chassis. These are well appointed and more expensive, but offer better handling and more amenities.

Roadtrek was recently purchased by the European motorhome builder Hymer, and are expanding their product line by offering new models in the US.

- **PleasureWay** – A well respected Canadian builder of high quality coaches. Often overlooked by Class B searches on the internet, but shouldn't be. They build a great coach, and sometimes you can find a bargain on a used one. If you're looking for a Class B, add PleasureWay to your stored internet searches.

- **Leisure Travel** – Another high quality Canadian builder of Class B motorhomes. I wouldn't hesitate to buy one of these if I found a good deal on one. Good floor plans and quality components. If looking for a Class B, add Leisure Travel to your stored internet searches, too.

- **Great West Vans** – Yet another Canadian builder of high quality Class B motorhomes. Has a reputation for solid wood throughout, great floor plans, excellent service after the sale. Not as well known as other class B builders, so you might be able to find a good deal on a used one. Note: No longer in business.

- **Airstream** – Yes, Airstream does build Class B motorhomes. The older ones are somewhat ungainly with high roofs that make them appear to be top heavy. These older ones are difficult to sell, and not much fun to drive in high winds.

The newer Airstream Class B's built on the Sprinter chassis are in high demand – selling new for over $100,000. Don't expect any bargains on these for a few years.

- **Coach House** – Coach House now builds only top of the line Class B+ motorhomes, but prior to moving to Class B+, they did build a very good Class B motorhome, up til 2001. These older units can sometimes be found at great prices.

- **Coachmen** – You'll find some older Coachmen Class B motorhomes in your searches, and among them you might discover the Coachmen StarFlight – which is a pretty nice motorhome for its age. If you can find one at the right price – under $8,000 – it can be a good deal.

- **Gulf Stream** – Their Vista Cruiser Class B van is Sprinter based, with the Mercedes diesel motor, and because of that, they fall into the high demand Sprinter price category.

  Gulf Stream has some build quality issues in their lower priced units, so look carefully before buying.

- **Sportsmobile** – a custom class B builder specializing in building coaches for the outdoor enthusiast. Almost all are custom, which means interiors will vary from unit to unit. Available with raised roofs or pop-tops. Four wheel drive units are one of their specialties.

- **Winnebago Rialta** – Is it a Class B, B+ or C? No one seems to know for sure. These vans were built on the VW Eurovan chassis, and had an appealing exterior design. Their best feature is the claimed fuel mileage of 15 to 17mpg. But their low interior ceiling height, the fold-out-of-the-wall bathroom, and 'always in the way' floor transmission mounted shifter turns off a lot of buyers.

  It's been more than fifteen years since VW ceased production of the Eurovan, so getting parts and service on a Rialta is becoming a major problem. Transmission issues are frequent and expensive. I would not recommend buying one.

The realities of motorhome fuel mileage

These days, with uncertainty about long term fuel prices, motorhome buyers are often concerned with how many miles per gallon a motorhome might get.

It is a very reasonable concern – as some motorhomes will only get 6 to 8 miles per gallon.

The reality is, if you only drive your motorhome three thousand miles per year (which is the average), miles per gallon won't make a huge difference in the long run.

But if you plan to put a lot of miles on your coach each year, the fuel costs can be significant.

When it comes to fuel mileage, here's what you can expect:

- Most gas **Class A coaches** powered by the Ford Triton V10 motor will get 7 to 10 miles per gallon, depending on how they are driven. Fuel mileage goes down at higher speed and in mountainous terrain or driving with a headwind.

- Most gas **Class C coaches** powered by either big block Ford or Chevy motors will get 8 to 11 miles per gallon.

- Most gas **Class B+** coaches powered by either Ford or Chevy motors will get 8 to 13 miles per gallon.

- Most **Class B+ motorhomes with the Mercedes 5** cylinder diesel motor will get 15 to 18 mpg.

- Most Class **B+ motorhomes with the Mercedes 6** cylinder diesel motor will get 12 to 15 mpg.

- Most gas **Class B camping vans** powered by Ford, Chevy or Dodge motors will get 13 to 15 mpg.

- Most **Class B camping vans with the Mercedes 5** cylinder diesel motor will get 18 to 23 mpg.

- If your goal is to get the absolute best fuel mileage in any motorhome, **simply keep the speed under 62 miles per hour**. At higher speeds the wind resistance puts a higher demand on the engine which requires more fuel.

- Driving 65 mph will drop fuel mileage by 20%.

- Driving 70 mph will drop fuel mileage by 40% (except in large diesel pushers).

Fuel mileage observations

If you get 10 mpg and drive three thousand miles per year, you'll use three hundred gallons of fuel.

If fuel costs $3.00 a gallon, your fuel costs will be 300 X 3 or $900 a year.

If you have a coach that gets 50% better mpg – say 15 mpg – and you drive the same three thousand miles per year, you'll use

200 gallons of fuel.

If that fuel costs $3.00 a gallon, your fuel costs will be 200 X 3 = $600.

So if you buy a motorhome that gets 50% better than the average of 10mpg, and drive the average three thousand miles per year, you'll save $300 in annual fuel costs.

But to get that higher mpg, you'll have to drive a much smaller Class B coach, and have to pay a substantial premium for the diesel motor and its required maintenance.

Even though it doesn't sound logical, the reality is, unless you drive many thousands of miles a year, the mpg you get in your motorhome really doesn't matter much.

In most cases, your motorhome will save you far more in motel room, restaurant and other travel expenses than any extra fuel costs due to mpg.

You've finally bought one . . .

After you purchase your motorhome and get it back to your residence, you'll probably be anxious to take it camping.

Before you do that, you'll want to stock your motorhome with the basic items that make a good trip.

Basic Items your motorhome will need

☐ A **power cord** to connect to campground shore power (30 or 50 amp depending on your coach)

☐ A new **fresh water hose** to connect to campground water

☐ A sturdy new **sewer hose** (don't rely on an old or cheap one). I prefer two fifteen foot sections of a Camco RhinoFlex hose (find on Amazon).

☐ RV friendly **toilet paper** (get Angel Soft or other septic safe tissue)

❏ **Flashlight**(s)

❏ **Basic tool kit** (screwdriver, pliers, small socket set, fuses, voltage meter, adjustable wrench)

❏ First Aid Kit

❏ Tire air pressure gauge

❏ Blankets, pillows, sheets

❏ Food and cooking supplies

❏ GPS or maps

As mentioned in a previous chapter, I recommend signing up with the Good Sams Club Emergency Road Service plan. This service, which is available for new members for under $70 a year, provides emergency road service, should your motorhome break down on the road. It includes a 24-hour toll free hotline, free unlimited towing, flat tire, lock out and fuel and fluid service.

Details: https://www.goodsamroadside.com/

On your first trip out, you'll probably find a few things that need to be fixed, some squeaks that need attention, and you'll discover items you'll want to bring on your next trip. This is to be expected whether you have a brand new motorhome or a used one.

You'll want make a list of these things while you're camping so you'll remember to bring them with you next time.

As mentioned earlier in this book, owning a motor-home gives you the freedom to travel and gives you the opportunity to create adventures you and your family will cherish forever.

If you follow what you've learned within these pages, you should be able to find the perfect motorhome for your needs, at a price you'll be comfortable paying.

And who knows, maybe one of these days we'll meet up in a campground, and you can show me what you bought.

Safe travels.

Bill Myers

Motorhome Resources

http://www.rv.net/forum/

http://motors.shop.ebay.com/RVs-and-Campers-/50054/i.html

http://www.rvtrader.com/

http://www.rvt.com/

http://www.roadtrekchapter.org/roadtreksforsale.htm

http://www.carfax.com/

http://rvs.oodle.com/used-rvs/for-sale/

http://www.campingworld.com/

http://www.goodsamclub.com/

http://groups.yahoo.com/

http://rvtravel.com/

http://www.goodsamers.com/

Definitions

Backup Monitor – camera in the back of a motorhome used to aid the driver in backing up the motorhome. It has a monitor upfront on or near the dashboard where it can be viewed by the driver.

Basement Storage – storage areas or compartments below the floor of a motorhome. Access to these areas is from the outside of the RV. Pass through storage means that the space goes from one side of the motorhome to the other with no division and can be accessed from either side.

Base Plate – If you have a tow vehicle, it'll need a base plate on the front so you can attach it to the tow bar on your motorhome. A base plate will cost at least $600.

Boon Docking – also known as 'dry camping.' Refers to camping without any hookups to electricity, sewer or water. Uses RV batteries for electric and fresh water from the holding tank.

Brake Controller – electronic controller in the tow vehicle within reach of the driver. It activates the trailer brakes when the tow vehicle brakes are applied. There is also a manual override that activates the trailer brakes without the tow vehicle brakes.

Chassis – the base that supports the body and engine of a motorhome.

Coach – refers to either the entire motorhome, or just the section behind the drivers area.

Converter – electrical device that converts 120-volt AC power to 12-volt DC power. Almost everything in an RV operates on 12-volt DC power that is supplied by a battery; exceptions include the roof AC, microwave, TV, and refrigerator (when not run on propane during travel).

Diesel Pusher – a motorhome with a diesel engine mounted in the rear.

Dinghy – refers to a vehicle that is towed with your motorhome. Also called a Toad.

Dry Bath - a bathroom where the shower and toilet are separate. As opposed to a wet bath where the toilet is part of the shower stall. A dry bath has more room and is usually preferred.

Dry Camping – also known as 'boon docking.' Refers to camping without any hookup to electricity, sewer or water. Uses RV batteries for electric and fresh water from the holding tank

Ducted AC – Air conditioning that is delivered throughout the RV via built-in duct work, usually in the ceiling.

Ducted Heat – Heat that is delivered throughout the RV via built-in duct work, usually in the floor.

Dump Station – facility for emptying black water and gray water holding tanks. Empty the black water tank first, then the gray water dump will help flush and initially rinse the dump hoses.

Full Time RV'ers – refers to people who live in their motorhomes full-time, or at least the majority of the time.

Generator – a device that is powered by gas or diesel or propane for generating 120 volt AC electricity. Used when not connected to shore power.

Hookups – Electric, water and sewer connections found at campgrounds.

Holding Tanks:

- **Fresh water tank** – for storage of fresh water for drinking, flushing and showers

- **Grey water tank** – holds waste water from sinks and shower

- **Black water tank** – holds waste water from toilet

Inverter – electrical device that converts 12-volt DC power into 120-volt AC power.

Leveling Jacks – optional jacks used to level RV when camped on an uneven surface. Some are manual, others are powered.

Pull-Through – refers to a camp site where you are able to pull through while setting up—no backing to get in or out required.

Roof AC – Roof mounted unit that provides air conditioning at that location only (it is not ducted throughout the unit.

Shore Power – electric power provided externally by connecting a power cable from the RV to camp site power source.

Slide Out/Slide Room – an area in your RV that slides out to allow additional living space.

Toad or Towed – refers to a vehicle that is towed with your motorhome. Also called a Dinghy.

Weights:

- **GVWR** – stands for Gross Vehicle Weight Rating. Refers to the manufacturer's maximum load weight allowed for the vehicle. This includes the weight of the vehicle plus the fuel, water, propane, supplies and passengers.

- **CCC** – Combined Cargo Capacity. The maximum weight of supplies and cargo that can be added to the RV. Equal to or less than GVWR minus UVW, full fresh water weight and full LP gas weight. The term CCC is replacing NCC in new RVs.

- **NCC** – Net Carrying Capacity, also called Payload Capacity. Refers to the maximum weight of the fuel, water, propane, supplies and passengers that can be added to an RV without exceeding the GVWR. See also CCC.

- **Dry Weight** – refers to the weight of the RV with no fuel, no fresh water, no propane, no supplies and no passengers. Also called UVW or Unloaded Vehicle Weight. This does not include dealer installed options.

- **GCWR** – stands for Gross Combined Weight Rating. Refers to the manufacturer's maximum load weight allowed for the trailer and tow vehicle. This includes the weight of the tow vehicle, and the trailer with all of their contents, including fuel, water, propane, supplies and passengers.

- **GAWR** – stands for Gross Axle Weight Rating. Refers to the manufacturer's maximum allowable weight on an individual axle. If an axle has a 3000-lb. GAWR and the RV has two axles, then the RV would have a GVWR of 6000 lbs.

- **Hitch Weight** – amount of a trailer's weight that rests on the tow vehicle's hitch. Usually 10% to 15% of the total weight of a travel trailer; usually 15% to 20% of the total weight of a fifth wheel

- **Wet Weight** – refers to the weight of your RV with the fuel, freshwater and propane tanks full.

Wet Bath – a bathroom where the shower and toilet are combined into one unit. As opposed to a dry bath where the shower stall is separate from the toilet. Wet bath's main benefit is saving space. The main drawback is very cramped, and the toilet is in the shower.

Wide Body – refers to an RV that is wider than the standard 8 feet. Wide body RVs are typically 8 feet 6 inches in width. More room inside, but can be more difficult to drive on narrow roads.

From the author

If you liked this book, please post a review at Amazon and let your friends know about the about it.

Also Available from Bill Myers

<u>Convert your Minivan into a Mini RV Camper:</u> How to convert a minivan into a comfortable minivan camper motorhome for under $200

<u>Mango Bob</u> (a novel about motor-home travel)
In this first book in the Mango Bob series, Walker has just lost his job, his wife has filed for divorce, and he's living in a tent down by the river.

Being ever resourceful, Walker swaps his truck for a motorhome (aka 'the Love Bus'), and agrees to drive it cross-country to sleepy Englewood Florida so he can deliver a cat named Mango Bob to a woman he's never met.

Should be easy, right? Drive to Florida, hand over the cat, and then hang out on the beach.

Except there's an unsolved murder involving the Love Bus, the Mexican mafia, and a half million in missing gold coins. Add to the mix a trigger happy grandma, a team of bungling burglars, the hot chick with the kayak, the repo man, and you get a rollicking travel romp through the Sunshine State. A fun and fast read!

Mango Lucky

John Walker, newly divorced and out of a job, seems to be on a lucky streak. He's hit the lottery and living the good life in Florida with Mango Bob, the cat, in their motorhome, aka the 'Love Bus'.

All Walker wants to do is hang out with his new friend and landlord, the lovely but bossy Sarah, and enjoy the laid back lifestyle in Englewood, a small Gulf Coast town.

But things get complicated when Sarah sends Walker and Mango Bob on a road trip to Florida's Treasure Coast, with instructions to find long-lost pirate's gold hidden beneath the sands.

Walker is soon caught up in a deadly storm that brings with it a gun-toting mystery woman whose secrets could change Walker's life forever. Helping Walker dig his way out of danger is Jake the Wonder Dog, whose hidden talents can't save Walker from his many new armed and slightly dangerous friends.

Also in the Mango Bob series:

Mango Bay

Mango Glades

Mango Key

Mango Blues

Made in the USA
Columbia, SC
05 June 2020